the difference is delicious!®

Simple & Delicious
Meals in Minutes

Meals in Minutes

The everyday drama—a performance that plays week after week in homes across America. Unfortunately, mealtime gets no special recognition in this hectic act, with "gourmet" starring only on special occasions.

Lawry's applauds you for making it through the "everydays!" With Lawry's *Simple & Delicious—Meals in Minutes* cookbook, everyday mealtime, too, can earn applause—365 days of the year.

This Lawry's collection offers more than 95 delicious, time-saving recipes sure to spice up your everyday routine. And we're not just talking uninspired spaghetti and boring chicken breasts!

In this new, innovative publication, Lawry's features dishes from regional and ethnic cuisines, casual family favorites as well as fare made popular by today's trendiest restaurants. Each deliciously different recipe is everyday-approved with preparation time for most recipes clocking in at 30 minutes or less. Plus, many dishes can be prepared ahead of time to be served later.

With these irresistible recipes and Lawry's full line of flavorful seasonings, you can simply say goodbye to those everyday meal-planning blahs. Lawry's Spice Blends, Spices & Seasoning Blends, Fruit Juice Marinades and Classic Salad Dressings make easy-to-prepare gourmet meals a breeze.

We appreciate and welcome your comments and requests. If you'd like more information from Lawry's, please call Lawry's Consumer Services at 1-800-9-LAWRYS between 8:30 a.m. and 4:00 p.m. E.S.T.

LAWRY'S SEASONED SALT

Lawry's Seasoned Salt has been shaking on delicious flavor in homes across the country for years. Lawry's Seasoned Salt, the original seasoned salt, is a unique blend of herbs, spices and salt that adds flavor and excitement that ordinary table salt cannot match! Use Lawry's Seasoned Salt as your secret ingredient and everyone will be asking for the recipe. Read on for some favorite uses.

- Use Lawry's Seasoned Salt instead of regular table salt and taste the difference.
- When grilling, shake on hamburgers, chicken, steak, seafood and vegetables.
- Shake Lawry's Seasoned Salt on turkey for mouthwatering flavor and a touch of color.
- Shake onto French fries and popcorn for a delicious change of pace.
- For a savory taste, add Lawry's Seasoned Salt to baked chicken, pork chops or any casserole.
- Add Lawry's Seasoned Salt to your next breading or coating mix.
- Use to enhance the flavor of soups, gravies, stews or casseroles.
- Stir into sautéed vegetables or mashed potatoes.

DIJON BABY BACK BARBECUED RIBS

The secret to succulent flavor is knowing which barbecue sauce to use.

2 to 3 teaspoons Lawry's Seasoned
   Salt
4 pounds pork baby back ribs

1 bottle (12 ounces) Lawry's Dijon
   & Honey Barbecue Sauce

Sprinkle Seasoned Salt onto both sides of ribs. In resealable bag or shallow glass baking dish, place ribs; seal bag or cover dish. Refrigerate at least 2 hours. Heat grill. Grill ribs, 4 to 5 inches from heat source, 45 to 60 minutes or until ribs are tender, turning and basting with Dijon & Honey Barbecue Sauce after 30 minutes. *Makes 4 to 6 servings*

PRESENTATION: Cut ribs into 3-bone portions to serve.

HINT: Ribs may be baked in 375°F oven 45 to 60 minutes or until ribs are tender, turning and basting with sauce every 10 minutes.

STEAK FAJITAS SUPREMA

Create a festive meal the whole family will enjoy!

2 tablespoons vegetable oil,
   divided
1 medium-sized red bell pepper,
   thinly sliced
1 medium onion, very thinly sliced
1 pound beef sirloin steak, thinly
   sliced
1 package (1.27 ounces) Lawry's
   Spices & Seasonings for
   Fajitas

¼ cup water
1 can (15 ounces) pinto beans,
   drained
6 medium flour *or* corn tortillas
1 cup (4 ounces) shredded
   Cheddar cheese (optional)
Salsa (optional)
Dairy sour cream (optional)
Sliced peeled avocado (optional)

In large skillet, heat 1 tablespoon oil. Add bell pepper and onion; sauté until crisp-tender. Remove vegetables from skillet; set aside. In same skillet, heat remaining 1 tablespoon oil. Add meat. Cook 5 to 7 minutes or to desired doneness; drain fat. Add Spices & Seasonings for Fajitas, water and pinto beans; blend well. Bring to a boil. Reduce heat to low; simmer, uncovered, 3 to 5 minutes or until thoroughly heated, stirring occasionally. Return vegetables to skillet; heat 1 minute. *Makes 4 to 6 servings*

PRESENTATION: Serve in warm tortillas. If desired, add shredded Cheddar cheese, salsa, sour cream and avocado to the inside for extra flavor.

HINT: Partially frozen meat is easier to slice thinly.

Dijon Baby Back Barbecued Ribs

LAWRY'S TACO SPICES & SEASONINGS

Enjoy the flavor of Taco Spices & Seasonings in many ways. Try this perfectly blended Mexican seasoning blend as a base for all your Mexican foods or just use to add zip to your favorite dishes. Following are a few ideas:

- Stir Taco Spices & Seasonings into coating mix for chicken or fish.
- Season enchilada fillings with Taco Spices & Seasonings for extra flavor.
- Season hot cooked ground beef or chicken with Taco Spices & Seasonings and toss with torn lettuce, chopped tomatoes, pitted ripe olives and tortilla chips for a delicious taco salad.
- Mix refried beans or rice into cooked ground beef or chicken that has been seasoned with Taco Spices & Seasonings. Place in warm flour tortillas and top with shredded cheese and salsa for great burritos.
- Mix 1 package (1.25 ounces) Taco Spices & Seasonings with 1 container (16 ounces) dairy sour cream for an easy crowd-pleasing Mexican-style chip or vegetable dip.
- Place cooked ground beef seasoned with Taco Spices & Seasonings over a bed of crisp tortilla chips. Top with shredded Cheddar cheese; place under broiler to melt. Top with sour cream and salsa for one-of-a-kind nachos.

*Above is only a representative sample of Lawry's Foods products. For full product listing, contact Lawry's Consumer Services at 1-800-9-LAWRYS.

ENTRÉES

It's easy to prepare nutritious, flavorful meals with Lawry's Spice Blends, Spices & Seasonings and Fruit Juice Marinades. Lean cuts of beef and pork, savory seafood and ever-popular chicken are transformed into exciting meals that make weekday cooking a breeze. Try one of these delightful recipes tonight!

BEEF & PORK

STEAK AU POIVRE

This classic flamed dish is dramatic to prepare at the table.

1 tablespoon Lawry's Seasoned Pepper
2 teaspoons Lawry's Seasoned Salt
1 (2½-pound) beef sirloin roast or steak, 2 inches thick
2 tablespoons butter
2 tablespoons olive oil
¼ cup dry white wine
2 tablespoons beef consommé *or* bouillon
¼ cup cognac *or* brandy

Press Seasoned Pepper and Seasoned Salt into both sides of steak with back of spoon. In large skillet, heat butter and oil. Add steak; cook 8 to 10 minutes on each side or to desired doneness, adding more oil, if necessary. Remove steak from skillet to serving plate; set aside. Reduce heat to low. Add wine and consommé to skillet; heat until warmed. Turn off heat. Remove skillet from heat. Add cognac or brandy; carefully ignite. Pour flaming sauce over steak. Serve immediately. *Makes 4 to 6 servings*

PRESENTATION: Serve with sautéed mushrooms and steamed asparagus.

Steak au Poivre

CHILI CHIP PARTY PLATTER

A festive dish for all ages.

1 pound ground beef
1 medium onion, chopped
1 package (1.62 ounces) Lawry's
   Spices & Seasonings for Chili
1 can (6 ounces) tomato paste
1 cup water
1 bag (8 to 9 ounces) tortilla chips
   or corn chips

1½ cups (6 ounces) shredded
   Cheddar cheese
1 can (2¼ ounces) sliced pitted
   ripe olives, drained
½ cup sliced green onion

In medium skillet, brown ground beef until crumbly; drain. Add onion, Spices & Seasonings for Chili, tomato paste and water; blend well. Bring to a boil. Reduce heat to low; simmer, uncovered, 15 minutes, stirring occasionally. Serve over tortilla chips. Top with Cheddar cheese, olives and green onion.   *Makes 4 servings*

PRESENTATION: Serve with a cool beverage and sliced melon.

SMOKEHOUSE RED BEAN AND SAUSAGE CASSEROLE

A great dish for potluck dinners.

3 cups chopped onion
3 bacon slices, diced
1 medium-sized green bell pepper,
   chopped
1 cup chopped fresh parsley
1 pound smoked sausage, cut into
   ¼-inch slices
2 cans (15¼ ounces *each*) kidney
   beans, undrained

1 can (8 ounces) tomato sauce
1 tablespoon Worcestershire sauce
1 tablespoon Lawry's Seasoned
   Salt
¾ teaspoon hot pepper sauce
½ teaspoon Lawry's Garlic Powder
   with Parsley
3 cups hot cooked white rice

In Dutch oven or large saucepan, sauté onion and bacon until bacon is just crisp and onion is transparent; drain fat. Add remaining ingredients except rice; blend well. Bring to a boil. Reduce heat to low; simmer, uncovered, 20 minutes, stirring occasionally.   *Makes 8 servings*

PRESENTATION: Serve over rice; this is perfect with a green salad and crusty bread.

HINT: Use 1 bag (12 ounces) frozen chopped onion instead of fresh onion.

Chili Chip Party Platter

SATAY SKEWERS WITH SESAME

The flavor of Thailand in an easy-to-make sauce.

1½ cups dry roasted peanuts
⅔ cup seasoned rice vinegar
½ cup light corn syrup
½ cup soy sauce
2 tablespoons sesame oil
2 tablespoons minced fresh ginger
2 tablespoons chopped fresh
   cilantro

½ teaspoon Lawry's Garlic Powder
   with Parsley
½ teaspoon crushed red pepper
   flakes (optional)
1 pound beef sirloin steak *or*
   1 pound boneless chicken, cut
   into strips
Skewers

In food processor, place peanuts, rice vinegar and corn syrup. Process until peanuts are puréed. Add soy sauce, sesame oil, ginger, cilantro, Garlic Powder with Parsley and red pepper flakes. Pulse until mixture is blended; cover. Refrigerate at least 1 hour. Thread meat onto skewers; brush with half of the sauce. Grill or broil to desired doneness, turning and brushing frequently with remaining sauce. In small saucepan, warm any remaining sauce for dipping.   *Makes 4 servings*

PRESENTATION: Serve with hot cooked white rice and iced tea.

POLYNESIAN BURGERS

Teriyaki flavor shines through to provide a new twist to the flavor of hamburgers.

1 pound ground beef
½ cup diced green bell pepper
¼ cup Lawry's Teriyaki Marinade
   with Pineapple Juice

1 can (5¼ ounces) pineapple
   slices, drained
4 hamburger buns, onion flavored

In medium bowl, combine ground beef, bell pepper and Teriyaki Marinade with Pineapple Juice. Let stand 10 to 15 minutes. Shape meat into four patties. Grill or broil on both sides to desired doneness. Add pineapple slices to grill or broiler pan; heat just until browned.   *Makes 4 servings*

PRESENTATION: Serve burgers on toasted buns topped with pineapple slices.

HINT: For extra teriyaki flavor, brush buns with additional Lawry's Teriyaki Marinade with Pineapple Juice; grill or broil until lightly toasted.

Satay Skewers with Sesame

OPEN–FACED MESQUITE STEAK SANDWICHES

A robust sandwich delicious off the grill.

1 pound flank steak
½ cup Lawry's Mesquite Marinade with Lime Juice
8 slices sourdough bread *or* thin French bread
4 ounces refried beans

1 small red onion, thinly sliced
1 medium-sized green bell pepper, thinly sliced
½ cup chunky-style salsa
4 ounces Cheddar cheese, sliced

Pierce steak several times with fork; place in large resealable plastic bag or shallow glass baking dish. Pour Mesquite Marinade with Lime Juice over steak. Seal bag or cover dish. Refrigerate at least 30 minutes. Remove steak from marinade. Place on grill or rack of broiler pan. Grill or broil, 4 inches from heat source, 4 to 5 minutes on each side or to desired doneness. Thinly slice steak across the grain of meat; set aside. Spread bread slices with refried beans; cover with meat, onion and bell pepper. Top with salsa and cheese. Grill or broil 1 minute or just until cheese is melted.   *Makes 4 servings*

PRESENTATION: Serve warm with a crisp green salad or mixed vegetables.

SAVORY PORK ROAST

A delicious old-time favorite that will never go out of style.

2 tablespoons lemon juice
1 tablespoon olive oil
2 teaspoons Lawry's Seasoned Salt
1 teaspoon Lawry's Garlic Salt

1 teaspoon dried thyme, crushed
1 (5-pound) boneless pork roast
1 to 2 tablespoons all-purpose flour
½ cup water

In small bowl, combine lemon juice, oil, Seasoned Salt, Garlic Salt and thyme. In shallow roasting pan, place meat; brush with seasoning mixture. Bake, uncovered, in 350°F oven 2 hours or until internal meat temperature reaches 170°F. Remove meat to serving platter, reserving drippings in pan; keep meat warm. Combine flour and water; add to drippings in pan. Cook over medium heat until thickened, stirring constantly.

Makes 6 to 8 servings

PRESENTATION: Serve gravy over slices of roast—great with mashed potatoes.

Open-Faced Mesquite Steak Sandwiches

RED VINAIGRETTE MARINATED BEEF

Marinating adds extra flavor to beef.

1 bottle (8 ounces) Lawry's Classic
   Red Wine Vinaigrette with
   Cabernet Sauvignon Dressing
¾ teaspoon Lawry's Garlic Salt
½ teaspoon dried rosemary,
   crushed

½ teaspoon dried oregano, crushed
1½ pounds sirloin, round *or* flank
   steak

In large resealable plastic bag or shallow glass dish, combine Classic Red
Wine Vinaigrette, Garlic Salt, rosemary and oregano. Pierce steak several
times with fork. Add steak to marinade; seal bag or cover dish. Refrigerate at
least 1 hour, turning occasionally. Remove steak from marinade. Broil or
grill, 4 to 5 inches from heat source, to desired doneness.

Makes 4 servings

PRESENTATION: Thinly slice steak.

HINT: Toss any leftover cooked meat with greens, tomatoes, red onion and
extra Classic Red Wine Vinaigrette for a hearty salad.

MESQUITE–FILLED BURGERS

A hearty filling of cheese and onions adds a new twist to hamburgers.

1 pound ground beef
½ cup Lawry's Mesquite Marinade
   with Lime Juice
½ cup chopped green bell pepper
½ cup finely chopped onion
¼ cup unseasoned bread crumbs
½ teaspoon Lawry's Seasoned
   Pepper

½ cup (2 ounces) shredded
   Cheddar cheese
4 hamburger buns, toasted
   Lettuce leaves
   Tomato slices

In large bowl, combine ground beef, Mesquite Marinade with Lime Juice,
bell pepper, onion, bread crumbs and Seasoned Pepper. Let stand 20
minutes. Shape meat into eight thin patties. In center of each of four patties,
place a layer of cheese; top with remaining patties. Press edges tightly
together to seal. Broil, 4 inches from heat source, 5 to 8 minutes on each side
or to desired doneness.

Makes 4 servings

PRESENTATION: Serve burgers on toasted buns with lettuce and tomato.

HINT: Ground turkey is an excellent substitute for the ground beef.

Red Vinaigrette Marinated Beef

COWBOY BURGERS

Just the right burger for all your cowboys—big or little.

1 pound ground beef
½ teaspoon Lawry's Seasoned Salt
½ teaspoon Lawry's Seasoned Pepper
2 tablespoons *plus* 2 teaspoons butter or margarine
1 large onion, thinly sliced and separated into rings

1 package (1.25 ounces) Lawry's Taco Spices and Seasonings
4 slices Cheddar cheese
4 Kaiser rolls
Lettuce leaves
Tomato slices

In medium bowl, combine ground beef, Seasoned Salt and Seasoned Pepper; shape into four patties. Grill or broil to desired doneness (about 4 minutes on each side for rare). Meanwhile, in medium skillet, melt butter. Add onion and Taco Spices & Seasonings; blend well. Sauté until onion is tender and translucent. Top each patty with cheese. Return to grill or broiler until cheese is melted. On bottom half of each roll, place lettuce, tomato and patty; cover with onion and top half of roll.   *Makes 4 servings*

PRESENTATION: Serve with hot baked beans.

LAWRY'S HOME–BAKED RIBS

This recipe smells soooooo good! Better make extra for the neighbors.

2 tablespoons Lawry's Seasoned Salt
6 pounds lean baby back ribs
1½ cups lemon juice
½ bottle (3.5 ounces) liquid smoke

1 bottle (16 ounces) barbecue sauce
Syrup from 1 can (16 ounces) peaches* (about ½ cup)

Sprinkle Seasoned Salt onto both sides of ribs. In large resealable bag or shallow glass baking dish, place ribs. Combine lemon juice and liquid smoke; pour over ribs. Seal bag or cover dish. Marinate in refrigerator at least 2 hours or overnight, turning occasionally. Remove ribs from marinade. Place in shallow baking pan. Bake in 350°F oven 1 hour. Reduce oven temperature to 300°F. Combine barbecue sauce and peach syrup; pour over ribs. Bake 30 to 45 minutes longer or until ribs are tender.   *Makes 8 servings*

PRESENTATION: Serve with potato salad and lots of napkins.

*Peaches can be refrigerated for later use.

Cowboy Burger

BARBECUED PORK LOIN

An easy-to-make company dish.

2 teaspoons Lawry's Seasoned
  Salt
1 (3- to 3½-pound) boneless pork
  loin
1 cup orange juice
¼ cup soy sauce

1 teaspoon Lawry's Garlic Powder
  with Parsley
½ teaspoon Lawry's Seasoned
  Pepper
Vegetable oil
Fresh herb sprigs (garnish)

Sprinkle Seasoned Salt onto all sides of meat. In large resealable plastic bag or shallow glass baking dish, place meat; let stand 10 to 15 minutes. Combine orange juice, soy sauce, Garlic Powder with Parsley and Seasoned Pepper; pour over meat. Seal bag or cover dish. Refrigerate at least 2 hours or overnight, turning occasionally. Heat grill; brush with vegetable oil. Remove meat from marinade, reserving marinade. Add meat to grill; cook 30 minutes or until internal meat temperature reaches 170°F, turning and brushing frequently with reserved marinade. Remove meat from grill; let stand about 10 minutes before thinly slicing. Meanwhile, in small saucepan, bring reserved marinade to a boil; boil 1 minute. *Makes 6 servings*

PRESENTATION: Serve sliced meat with extra heated marinade poured over top. Garnish with fresh herb sprigs. Serve with steamed vegetables.

CONVENTIONAL DIRECTIONS: Marinate meat as directed. Remove meat from marinade, reserving marinade. Place meat in shallow roasting pan; brush with reserved marinade. Bake, uncovered, in 350°F oven 1 hour or until internal temperature reaches 170°F, brushing frequently with reserved marinade. Discard any remaining marinade.

GARLIC–PEPPER STEAK

A well-seasoned steak to serve family and friends.

1¼ teaspoons Lawry's Garlic
  Powder with Parsley
1¼ teaspoons Lawry's Seasoned
  Pepper

½ teaspoon Lawry's Seasoned Salt
1 pound sirloin steak

Combine Garlic Powder with Parsley, Seasoned Pepper and Seasoned Salt. Press seasoning mixture into both sides of steak with back of spoon. Let stand 30 minutes. Grill or broil as desired. *Makes 4 servings*

PRESENTATION: Serve with rice pilaf and a crisp green salad.

Barbecued Pork Loin

HERBED CITRUS CHOPS

Rosemary, Dijon and orange give exciting flavor to pork.

4 pork loin chops
¾ cup orange juice
3 tablespoons Lawry's Dijon &
   Honey Barbecue Sauce
2 tablespoons minced onion
1 teaspoon freshly grated orange
   peel

½ teaspoon dried rosemary,
   crushed
1 orange, sliced (garnish)
   Chopped fresh parsley (garnish)

Pierce pork chops several times with fork; place in large resealable plastic bag or shallow glass baking dish. In small bowl, combine orange juice, Dijon & Honey Barbecue Sauce, onion, orange peel and rosemary; pour over chops. Seal bag or cover dish. Refrigerate at least 30 minutes, turning occasionally. Remove chops from bag, reserving marinade. Grill or broil chops, 4 inches from heat source, 5 to 7 minutes on each side or until just slightly pink in center, brushing with reserved marinade halfway through cooking time.

Makes 4 servings

PRESENTATION: Garnish with orange slices and chopped parsley.

KIDS' TACO–MAC

A dish the children will be sure to enjoy!

1 pound ground beef
1 package (1.25 ounces) Lawry's
   Taco Spices & Seasonings
1 can (14½ ounces) diced
   tomatoes, undrained
1½ cups water
8 ounces uncooked macaroni *or*
   small spiral pasta

½ cup sliced celery
1 egg
⅓ cup milk
1 package (8½ ounces) corn
   muffin mix
½ cup (2 ounces) shredded
   Cheddar cheese

In medium skillet, brown ground beef until crumbly; drain. Blend in Taco Spices & Seasonings, tomatoes, water, macaroni and celery. Bring to a boil. Reduce heat to low; cover. Simmer 20 minutes, stirring occasionally. Spoon meat mixture into 2½-quart casserole dish; set aside. Heat oven to 400°F. In medium bowl, beat egg. Stir in milk. Add muffin mix; stir with fork just until muffin mix is moistened. Spoon half of the batter over meat mixture in dollops. Spoon remaining batter into 6 greased or paper-lined medium-sized muffin cups. Bake casserole and muffins 15 to 20 minutes or until golden.

Makes 6 to 8 servings

PRESENTATION: Sprinkle hot baked casserole with shredded Cheddar cheese before serving.

NOTE: Cool muffins completely. Wrap tightly and freeze for later use, if desired.

CALZONE MEXICANA

An Italian dish with a Mexican twist.

1 package (1.25 ounces) Lawry's
  Taco Spices & Seasonings
1 pound ground beef
¾ cup water
  All-purpose flour
1 pound frozen bread dough,
  thawed, *or* 2 cans (9 ounces
  each) refrigerated pizza dough

2 cups (8 ounces) shredded
  Monterey Jack cheese
1 can (4 ounces) diced green chiles,
  drained
  Dairy sour cream (garnish)
  Salsa (garnish)

Heat oven to 350°F. Prepare Taco Spices & Seasonings with ground beef and
water according to package directions; set aside. On floured board, roll out
dough to 14×8-inch rectangle. Spread taco meat mixture onto center of
dough, leaving 2-inch border. Layer cheese and chiles on top. Fold dough
lengthwise in half; pinch edges together to seal. Place on lightly greased
baking sheet. Bake, uncovered, 30 minutes or until golden brown.
Makes 4 to 6 servings

PRESENTATION: Cut into slices and top with sour cream and salsa, if
desired.

HINT: For extra flavor, brush top of calzone with beaten egg and lightly
sprinkle with cornmeal before baking.

VARIATION: For four individual calzones, cut rolled dough into four equal
rectangles. Fill and fold as directed above. Place on lightly greased baking
sheet. Bake at 350°F 20 minutes or until golden brown.

MARINATED BEEF TENDERLOIN

Excellent for special company or holiday meals.

¾ cup dry vermouth
¼ cup olive oil
¼ cup chopped shallots
1 teaspoon Lawry's Garlic Powder
  with Parsley
1 teaspoon dried rosemary

¾ teaspoon dried thyme, crushed
¾ teaspoon Lawry's Seasoned Salt
¾ teaspoon Lawry's Seasoned
  Pepper
1½ pounds beef tenderloin

In small bowl, combine all ingredients except meat. Pierce meat several
times with fork. In large resealable plastic bag or glass baking dish, place
meat and marinade. Seal bag or cover dish. Marinate in refrigerator at least
1 hour or overnight, turning occasionally. Bake at 400°F, uncovered, 50
minutes to 1 hour or until internal meat temperature reaches 180°F. Let
stand 5 minutes before slicing.   *Makes 4 to 6 servings*

PRESENTATION: Serve with garlic potatoes and your favorite vegetable.

GLAZED CITRUS CHICKEN

A fresh and tangy recipe for chicken.

4 boneless, skinless chicken breast
    halves (¾ to 1 pound)
2 medium oranges
2 medium lemons
2 medium limes
2 teaspoons Lawry's Seasoned
    Salt

2 teaspoons Lawry's Seasoned
    Pepper
1 can (12 ounces) apricot halves,
    drained
2 tablespoons brown sugar
1 tablespoon butter or margarine
    Dash of ground nutmeg

In 13×9-inch glass baking dish, place chicken. Cut 1½ oranges, lemons *and*
limes into thin slices; cover and set aside for garnish. Squeeze juice from
remaining fruit halves over chicken. Sprinkle Seasoned Salt and Seasoned
Pepper evenly over chicken; cover. Bake in 400°F oven 30 minutes.
Meanwhile, place apricots in blender; blend until smooth. In small saucepan,
combine puréed apricots, brown sugar, butter and nutmeg. Bring to a boil.
Reduce heat to low; cover. Simmer 5 minutes, stirring occasionally. Pour
over chicken. Bake, uncovered, an additional 10 minutes.

Makes 4 servings

PRESENTATION: Garnish with citrus slices.

GREEK–STYLE BAKED CHICKEN

A new twist to baked chicken.

3 to 3½ pounds chicken pieces
    (Best of Fryer)
¼ cup lemon juice
1 tablespoon dried oregano,
    crushed

1 teaspoon Lawry's Garlic Powder
    with Parsley
½ teaspoon Lawry's Seasoned Salt
½ teaspoon Lawry's Seasoned
    Pepper

Pierce chicken pieces several times with fork; place in large resealable plastic
bag or shallow dish. In small bowl, combine all remaining ingredients; pour
over chicken. Seal bag or cover dish. Refrigerate at least 30 minutes, turning
often. Remove chicken from marinade, reserving marinade. In 13×9-inch
baking dish, arrange chicken, skin side up. Brush with reserved marinade.
Bake, uncovered, in 400°F oven 40 to 45 minutes or until chicken is no
longer pink in center, basting frequently.

Makes 4 to 6 servings

PRESENTATION: Serve with garlic mashed potatoes.

Glazed Citrus Chicken

ROLLED MEXICAN CHICKEN

Serve this recipe sliced to show off the attractive spirals.

8 boneless, skinless chicken breast halves (2 pounds)
1 package (1.25 ounces) Lawry's Taco Spices & Seasonings, divided
1 cup (4 ounces) shredded Monterey Jack cheese

1 can (4 ounces) diced green chiles, drained
¼ cup butter or margarine, melted, *or* 1 to 2 egg whites, slightly beaten
1 bag (8 ounces) tortilla chips, crushed

Place chicken breasts between two sheets of waxed paper; pound to ⅛-inch thickness. In medium bowl, combine 1 tablespoon Taco Spices & Seasonings, cheese and green chiles. Spread equal amounts of cheese mixture onto chicken breasts. Roll up chicken tightly; secure with toothpick. In shallow baking dish, place butter. Roll each chicken bundle in melted butter. In second shallow dish or on plate, combine remaining Taco Spices & Seasonings and tortilla chips. Roll each chicken bundle in seasoned chips to coat; return to baking dish. Bake in 350°F oven 30 minutes or until juices run clear when chicken is cut. Remove from oven; let stand 5 minutes before slicing to serve. Garnish, if desired. *Makes 6 to 8 servings*

PRESENTATION: Serve with Mexicali Rice and Beans (page 81), if desired.

HAWAIIAN CHICKEN

Go Hawaiian!

4 boneless, skinless chicken breast halves (¾ to 1 pound)
½ to ¾ teaspoon Lawry's Garlic Salt
½ to ¾ teaspoon Lawry's Seasoned Pepper
2 tablespoons vegetable oil
½ cup thinly sliced onion
½ cup thinly sliced red *or* green bell pepper

1 cup pineapple juice
1 can (8 ounces) pineapple chunks, drained
¼ cup white vinegar
2 tablespoons *plus* 1½ teaspoons brown sugar
2 tablespoons cornstarch
2 tablespoons soy sauce
3 cups hot cooked rice

In shallow baking dish, place chicken. Sprinkle with Garlic Salt and Seasoned Pepper. Bake in 350°F oven 20 to 25 minutes or until no longer pink in center. Meanwhile, in large skillet, heat oil. Add onion and bell pepper; sauté until crisp-tender. Stir in pineapple juice, pineapple chunks, vinegar and brown sugar. In small bowl, combine cornstarch and soy sauce; add to skillet. Bring to a boil, stirring constantly. Reduce heat to low; simmer until thickened, stirring constantly. Serve over chicken.

Makes 4 servings

PRESENTATION: Serve over hot cooked rice.

Rolled Mexican Chicken with Mexicali Rice and Beans (page 81)

GRILLED CHICKEN PASTA TOSS

The flavors of herbs and garlic add incredible style to this pasta dish.

6 boneless, skinless chicken breast
  halves (about 1½ pounds)
1 bottle (12 ounces) Lawry's Herb
  & Garlic Marinade with
  Lemon Juice, divided
3 tablespoons vegetable oil,
  divided
1½ cups broccoli florets and sliced
  stems

1 cup Chinese pea pods
1 cup diagonally sliced carrots
1 can (2¼ ounces) sliced pitted
  ripe olives, drained
8 ounces fettuccine or linguine
  noodles, cooked, drained and
  kept hot

Preheat grill. Pierce chicken pieces several times with fork. In large resealable plastic bag or shallow glass dish, place chicken. Add 1 cup Lawry's Herb & Garlic Marinade with Lemon Juice; seal bag or cover dish. Refrigerate at least 30 minutes. Remove chicken from marinade, reserving marinade. Grill chicken, 5 inches from heat source, 5 to 7 minutes on each side or until no longer pink in center, brushing halfway through cooking time with reserved marinade. Remove chicken from grill; slice chicken. Cover and set aside. In medium skillet, heat 2 tablespoons oil. Add broccoli, pea pods and carrots; sauté until crisp-tender. In large bowl, combine sautéed vegetables, olives, hot noodles and chicken. In small bowl, combine remaining Herb & Garlic Marinade with Lemon Juice and remaining 1 tablespoon oil. Add just enough dressing to noodle mixture to coat; toss well. Serve with any remaining dressing, if desired.   *Makes 4 to 6 servings*

PRESENTATION: Sprinkle with chopped fresh parsley, if desired.

ITALIAN MARINATED CHICKEN

Salad dressings add extra flair to any side or main dish.

1 bottle (8 ounces) Lawry's Classic
  Italian with Aged Parmesan
  Dressing
2 tablespoons finely chopped onion
2 tablespoons lemon juice

¾ teaspoon Lawry's Seasoned
  Pepper
6 boneless, skinless chicken breast
  halves (about 1½ pounds)

In large resealable plastic bag or shallow glass dish, combine all ingredients except chicken. Pierce chicken several times with fork Add to marinade. Seal bag or cover dish. Refrigerate at least 1 hour, turning occasionally. Broil or grill as desired.   *Makes 6 to 8 servings*

PRESENTATION: Perfect served with any pasta or crisp green salad.

HINT: Chill leftover chicken and slice for use in salads or sandwiches.

Grilled Chicken Pasta Toss

SPINACH–STUFFED CHICKEN BREASTS

An excellent recipe to make ahead.

8 boneless, skinless chicken breast halves (about 2 pounds)
1 package (12 ounces) frozen spinach soufflé, thawed

½ cup Lawry's Dijon & Honey Barbecue Sauce
4 ounces cream cheese, softened
½ teaspoon paprika

With sharp knife, slit one side of each chicken breast to form a pocket. In medium bowl, combine all remaining ingredients except paprika. Spoon spinach mixture into pocket of each chicken breast. In 13×9-inch baking dish, arrange chicken breasts. Sprinkle with paprika. Bake, uncovered, in 350°F oven 35 to 40 minutes or until chicken is no longer pink in center. Garnish, if desired. *Makes 6 to 8 servings*

PRESENTATION: Serve by placing chicken breast on a seasoned rice mixture with whole baby carrots on the side.

GRILLED TURKEY CUTLETS WITH FRESH SALSA

A fresh and flavorful twist to classic turkey.

4 or 5 turkey cutlets (about 1¼ pounds)
1 bottle (12 ounces) Lawry's Herb & Garlic Marinade with Lemon Juice, divided
1 large tomato, chopped
¼ cup chopped mild green chile peppers *or* 1 can (2.25 ounces) diced green chiles, drained (optional)

¼ cup sliced green onion
1 tablespoon red wine vinegar
1 tablespoon chopped fresh cilantro
½ teaspoon Lawry's Garlic Salt
Flour tortillas, warmed

Preheat grill. Pierce turkey several times with fork; place in large resealable plastic bag or shallow glass dish. Add 1 cup Herb & Garlic Marinade with Lemon Juice; seal bag or cover dish. Refrigerate at least 30 minutes, turning occasionally. Meanwhile, prepare salsa by combining tomato, chile peppers, green onion, vinegar, cilantro, Garlic Salt and ¼ cup Herb & Garlic Marinade with Lemon Juice; cover. Refrigerate until ready to serve. Remove turkey from marinade. Grill, 5 inches from heat source, 7 to 10 minutes or until turkey is no longer pink in center, turning over at least once. Remove from grill; top with salsa. Serve with tortillas. *Makes 4 servings*

PRESENTATION: Serve this healthy entrée at your next barbecue party with lots of chips and guacamole.

Spinach-Stuffed Chicken Breast

TURKEY SCALOPPINE

A less expensive scaloppine recipe using turkey instead of veal.

1 pound turkey cutlets *or*
    4 boneless, skinless chicken
    breast halves (¾ to 1 pound)
2 tablespoons all-purpose flour
1½ teaspoons Lawry's Seasoned
    Salt, divided
1 teaspoon Lawry's Lemon Pepper
3 tablespoons olive oil, divided
1 medium-sized green bell pepper,
    cut into strips

1 cup sliced butternut squash *or*
    zucchini
½ cup sliced fresh mushrooms
1 teaspoon cornstarch
½ teaspoon Lawry's Garlic Powder
    with Parsley
¼ cup dry white wine
⅓ cup chicken broth
1 tablespoon *plus* 1½ teaspoons
    lemon juice

Place turkey between two sheets of waxed paper; pound to ⅛-inch thickness. In large resealable plastic bag, combine flour, ¾ teaspoon Seasoned Salt and Lemon Pepper. Add turkey, a few pieces at a time, to plastic bag; seal bag. Shake until well coated. In large skillet, heat 2 tablespoons oil. Add turkey; cook about 5 minutes on each side or until no longer pink in center. Remove from skillet; keep warm. In same skillet, heat remaining 1 tablespoon oil. Add bell pepper, squash and mushrooms; sauté until bell peppers are crisp-tender. Reduce heat to low. In small bowl, combine cornstarch, Garlic Powder with Parsley and remaining ¾ teaspoon Seasoned Salt; blend well. Stir in combined wine, broth and lemon juice. Add to skillet. Bring just to a boil, stirring constantly. Simmer 1 minute. Garnish, if desired.

Makes 4 servings

PRESENTATION: On platter, layer vegetables, turkey or chicken and top with sauce.

SESAME–ORANGE BARBECUE SKEWERS

A barbecue sauce with an Oriental flavor.

1 large orange
½ cup hoisin sauce
½ cup ketchup
¼ cup seasoned rice vinegar
¼ cup sesame oil
1 teaspoon toasted sesame seeds

½ teaspoon Lawry's Garlic Salt
6 boneless, skinless chicken breast
    halves (about 1½ pounds), cut
    into strips
Skewers

Cut orange in half; squeeze enough juice from one half to measure ¼ cup. Peel remaining orange half; chop enough fruit to measure 2 tablespoons. In small bowl, combine orange juice, chopped orange, hoisin, ketchup, vinegar, oil, sesame seeds and Garlic Salt. Cover and refrigerate at least 1 hour. Thread chicken onto skewers; brush with sauce. Grill or broil, 4 to 5 inches from heat source, 10 minutes or until chicken is no longer pink in center, brushing frequently with remaining sauce.

Makes 4 servings

PRESENTATION: Serve with rice and steamed vegetables.

CHICKEN TERIYAKI KABOBS

These grilled kabobs are especially delicious.

4 boneless, skinless chicken breast
    halves (¾ to 1 pound), cut into
    1-inch cubes
2 medium zucchini, cut into
    ½-inch-thick slices
1 medium-sized green bell pepper,
    cut into 1-inch squares
1 small red onion, cut into ½-inch
    cubes

Skewers
1 cup Lawry's Teriyaki Marinade
    with Pineapple Juice, divided
½ teaspoon Lawry's Seasoned
    Pepper
¼ teaspoon Lawry's Garlic Powder
    with Parsley

Preheat grill. Place chicken and vegetables on skewers, alternating chicken
with vegetables. Place in large shallow baking dish. Pour ¾ cup Teriyaki
Marinade with Pineapple Juice over kabobs. Turn kabobs over to coat all
sides. Cover dish. Refrigerate at least 30 minutes, turning once. Remove
skewers from marinade; discard marinade. Sprinkle skewers with Seasoned
Pepper and Garlic Powder with Parsley. Grill, 4 to 5 inches from heat source,
10 to 12 minutes or until chicken is no longer pink in center, turning and
brushing occasionally with remaining ¼ cup Teriyaki Marinade with
Pineapple Juice. *Makes 6 servings*

PRESENTATION: Great served with steamed rice or baked potatoes.

FIESTA CHICKEN AND RICE

An easy one-skillet dish, perfect for the whole family.

1 tablespoon vegetable oil
¾ cup chopped onion
4 boneless, skinless chicken breast
    halves (¾ to 1 pound), cut into
    2-inch strips
1 can (14½ ounces) chicken broth
1 cup sliced fresh mushrooms
¾ cup uncooked long-grain rice
½ cup dry white wine
1 teaspoon Lawry's Garlic Powder
    with Parsley

½ teaspoon Lawry's Seasoned
    Pepper
⅛ teaspoon ground saffron *or*
    turmeric
1 bag (16 ounces) frozen mixed
    vegetables, thawed and
    drained
1 jar (2 ounces) sliced pimiento,
    drained

In large skillet, heat oil. Add onion; sauté 5 minutes. Add chicken; cook 5
minutes or just until chicken is browned on all sides, stirring occasionally.
Stir in broth, mushrooms, rice, wine, Garlic Powder with Parsley, Seasoned
Pepper and saffron. Bring to a boil. Reduce heat to low; cover. Simmer 20
minutes or until rice is tender and liquid is absorbed. Stir in mixed
vegetables and pimiento; heat through, about 5 minutes.

Makes 4 servings

PRESENTATION: For added color, sprinkle finished dish with grated
Parmesan cheese and chopped fresh parsley, if desired.

CREOLE CHICKEN

A Southern recipe with worldwide appeal.

1 tablespoon *plus* 1½ teaspoons
   vegetable oil
2½ to 3 pounds chicken pieces
   (Best of Fryer)
1 tablespoon butter or margarine
1 medium onion, thinly sliced
2 teaspoons Lawry's Garlic
   Powder with Parsley
1½ teaspoons Lawry's Seasoned
   Salt

1 teaspoon Lawry's Seasoned
   Pepper
1 can (8 ounces) tomato sauce
½ cup red wine
3 medium tomatoes, chopped
2 medium-sized red and/or green
   bell peppers, sliced into strips
3 cups hot cooked white rice
   Fresh cilantro leaves (garnish)

In large skillet, heat oil. Add chicken; cook until browned on all sides. Remove chicken from skillet; set aside. In same skillet, heat butter. Add onion; sauté until tender. Add Garlic Powder with Parsley, Seasoned Salt and Seasoned Pepper. Return chicken to skillet. Add all remaining ingredients except rice and cilantro. Reduce heat to low; cover. Simmer 30 to 40 minutes or until chicken is no longer pink in center. Serve over rice.

Makes 4 to 6 servings

PRESENTATION: Garnish with cilantro leaves and serve with Lipton iced tea.

QUICK GRILLED TURKEY

Now there is an easier and quicker way to grill your turkey.

1 (12-pound) turkey, thawed
¼ cup olive oil
   Lawry's Seasoned Salt

Lawry's Seasoned Pepper
Lawry's Garlic Powder with
   Parsley

Preheat grill. Place turkey, breast side down, in large shallow microwave-safe dish. Brush with olive oil; sprinkle generously with Seasoned Salt and Seasoned Pepper. Microwave on HIGH 12 minutes. Turn dish; baste turkey with drippings in dish. Microwave on MEDIUM-HIGH (75%) 20 to 25 minutes or until internal temperature reaches 135°F, turning dish after 13 minutes. Sprinkle with Seasoned Salt and Garlic Powder with Parsley. Place turkey on large sheet of heavy-duty aluminum foil. Insert meat thermometer into thickest part of turkey breast, making sure thermometer does not touch any bones. Wrap in foil, crimping foil around thermometer, making sure foil does not touch rod of thermometer. (Or, if using a turkey with a pop-up thermometer, make sure you can easily open foil to check for presence of thermometer during grilling.) Place turkey, breast side up, on grill. Grill 13 to 15 minutes per pound (2½ to 3 hours) or until internal temperature is 185°F and juices run clear.

Makes 8 to 10 servings

PRESENTATION: Delicious with your favorite stuffing or mashed potatoes.

Creole Chicken

LEMON CHICKEN HERB STIR-FRY

A touch of lemon and herb give a unique flavor to this stir-fry.

1 tablespoon *plus* 1½ teaspoons peanut oil
2 green onions, cut into 1-inch pieces
1 large carrot, julienne cut
1 pound boneless, skinless chicken breast halves *or* boneless pork loin, cut into strips
2 cups broccoli florets
1 can (8 ounces) bamboo shoots, drained

1 cup Lawry's Herb & Garlic Marinade with Lemon Juice
1 tablespoon soy sauce
½ teaspoon arrowroot
1 can (11 ounces) mandarin orange segments, drained (optional)
1 tablespoon sesame seeds
3 cups hot cooked rice

In large wok or skillet, heat oil. Add onion and carrot; sauté 5 minutes. Add chicken, broccoli and bamboo shoots; stir-fry 7 to 9 minutes until chicken is no longer pink in center. In small bowl, whisk together Herb & Garlic Marinade with Lemon Juice, soy sauce and arrowroot. Add to skillet; continue cooking, stirring constantly, until sauce forms glaze. Stir in orange segments. Sprinkle with sesame seeds. *Makes 6 servings*

PRESENTATION: Serve over hot rice.

SOUTHWEST CHICKEN SANDWICHES

Mesquite marinade and salsa combine to make a great chicken sandwich.

4 boneless, skinless chicken breast halves (¾ to 1 pound)
¾ cup Lawry's Mesquite Marinade with Lime Juice
½ teaspoon Lawry's Garlic Powder with Parsley
½ cup chunky-style salsa

¼ cup mayonnaise
4 sandwich rolls, split
Lettuce leaves
1 tomato, thinly sliced
1 avocado, peeled, pitted and thinly sliced

Pierce chicken several times with fork. Place in large resealable plastic bag or shallow dish. In small bowl, combine Mesquite Marinade with Lime Juice and Garlic Powder with Parsley. Add to chicken; seal bag or cover dish. Refrigerate at least 30 minutes. Remove chicken from marinade; discard marinade. Broil or grill chicken breasts, 5 inches from heat source, 7 to 10 minutes on each side or until chicken is no longer pink in center. In small bowl, combine salsa and mayonnaise; spread onto cut sides of rolls. Top bottom half of each roll with lettuce, chicken, tomato and avocado; cover with top half of roll. *Makes 4 servings*

PRESENTATION: Serve with fresh fruit, chips and salsa.

NOTE: For extra flavor, brush chicken with additional Mesquite Marinade with Lime Juice while cooking.

Lemon Chicken Herb Stir-Fry

CHICKEN AND BLACK BEAN CHILI

Give your chili its own personal touch.

1 tablespoon vegetable oil
1 medium onion, chopped
4 boneless, skinless chicken breast halves (¾ to 1 pound), cooked and cut into strips
2 cans (14½ ounces *each*) diced tomatoes, undrained
1 can (15 ounces) black beans, rinsed and drained
1 can (4 ounces) diced green chiles, drained

½ cup water
½ teaspoon Lawry's Garlic Powder with Parsley
1 package (1.62 ounces) Lawry's Spices & Seasonings for Chili
½ teaspoon hot pepper sauce (optional)
1 tablespoon chopped fresh cilantro

In large, deep skillet, heat oil. Add onion; sauté until tender and translucent. Add all remaining ingredients except cilantro. Bring to a boil. Reduce heat to low; simmer, uncovered, 20 minutes, stirring occasionally. Stir in cilantro.

Makes 5½ cups

PRESENTATION: Serve with dairy sour cream and tortilla chips. Diced avocados make a great garnish, too.

VARIATION: Substitute 1½ pounds ground turkey or chicken, browned in 1 tablespoon oil, for shredded chicken.

SPICY FRIED CHICKEN

Give your fried chicken a new twist!

3 to 3½ pounds chicken pieces, (Best of Fryer)
⅓ cup all-purpose flour
2 tablespoons cornmeal
1 teaspoon baking powder
1 package (1.25 ounces) Lawry's Taco Spices & Seasonings
1¼ teaspoons Lawry's Seasoned Salt

1 teaspoon paprika
¾ teaspoon cayenne pepper
½ teaspoon Lawry's Seasoned Pepper
¼ cup butter *or* shortening, melted
2 tablespoons lemon juice

Pierce chicken pieces several times with fork. In large resealable plastic bag, combine flour, cornmeal, baking powder, Taco Spices & Seasonings, Seasoned Salt, paprika, cayenne pepper and Seasoned Pepper. Add chicken, a few pieces at a time, to plastic bag; seal bag. Shake until well coated. Place chicken in shallow baking pan. Combine butter and lemon juice; drizzle over chicken. Bake in 400°F oven 1 hour or until chicken is no longer pink in center.

Makes 6 to 8 servings

PRESENTATION: Serve with hot buttered corn on the cob and lots of napkins.

Chicken and Black Bean Chili

CARIBBEAN JERK–STYLE CHICKEN

A Caribbean specialty you can do at home.

3 tablespoons chopped onion
2 tablespoons dried thyme,
  crushed
1 tablespoon *plus* 1½ teaspoons
  sugar
1 tablespoon Lawry's Seasoned
  Salt
1 tablespoon Lawry's Seasoned
  Pepper
2 teaspoons ground allspice

½ teaspoon ground cinnamon
¼ teaspoon hot pepper sauce
¼ teaspoon Lawry's Garlic Powder
  with Parsley
⅛ teaspoon ground ginger
6 boneless, skinless chicken breast
  halves (about 1½ pounds)
1 tablespoon margarine or butter
1 tablespoon vegetable oil

In small bowl, combine onion, thyme, sugar, Seasoned Salt, Seasoned Pepper, allspice, cinnamon, hot pepper sauce, Garlic Powder with Parsley and ginger. Pierce chicken breasts several times with fork. Place chicken in shallow dish. Spoon seasoning mixture over both sides of chicken, pressing into chicken with back of spoon; cover. Refrigerate at least 20 minutes. In large skillet, over medium-high heat, heat margarine and oil. Add chicken; cook 5 to 7 minutes on each side or until no longer pink in center. Garnish, if desired. *Makes 4 to 6 servings*

PRESENTATION: Serve with fresh coleslaw or a cool marinated bell pepper salad.

CILANTRO GINGER CHICKEN

Chicken with the fresh taste of cilantro.

4 boneless chicken breast halves
  (¾ to 1 pound)
½ cup Lawry's Teriyaki Marinade
  with Pineapple Juice
1 can (8 ounces) crushed
  pineapple, undrained

2 tablespoons chopped fresh
  cilantro
½ teaspoon Lawry's Garlic Powder
  with Parsley
½ teaspoon fresh minced ginger

Pierce chicken several times with fork. Place in large resealable plastic bag or shallow glass dish. In small bowl, combine remaining ingredients; pour over chicken. Seal bag or cover dish. Refrigerate at least 1 hour or overnight. Remove chicken from marinade, reserving ½ cup marinade. In large skillet, place chicken breasts and reserved marinade; cover. Cook over medium heat 15 to 17 minutes or until chicken is no longer pink in center, turning over after 8 minutes. *Makes 4 servings*

PRESENTATION: Also great grilled or broiled.

Caribbean Jerk-Style Chicken

TEX–MEX CHICKEN FAJITAS

Lime adds just the right tang!

6 boneless, skinless chicken breast
  halves (about 1½ pounds), cut
  into strips
½ cup Lawry's Mesquite Marinade
  with Lime Juice*
3 tablespoons *plus* 1½ teaspoons
  vegetable oil, divided
1 small onion, sliced and separated
  into rings
1 medium-sized green bell pepper,
  cut into strips

¾ teaspoon Lawry's Garlic Powder
  with Parsley
½ teaspoon hot pepper sauce
1 medium tomato, cut into wedges
2 tablespoons chopped fresh
  cilantro
Flour tortillas, warmed
1 medium lime, cut into wedges

Pierce chicken several times with fork; place in large resealable plastic bag or bowl. Pour Mesquite Marinade with Lime Juice over chicken; seal bag or cover bowl. Refrigerate at least 30 minutes. Heat 1 tablespoon plus 1½ teaspoons oil in large skillet. Add onion, bell pepper, Garlic Powder with Parsley and hot pepper sauce; sauté 5 to 7 minutes or until onion is crisp-tender. Remove vegetable mixture from skillet; set aside. Heat remaining 2 tablespoons oil in same skillet. Add chicken; sauté 8 to 10 minutes or until chicken is no longer pink in center, stirring frequently. Return vegetable mixture to skillet with tomato and cilantro; heat through.

Makes 4 to 6 servings

PRESENTATION: Serve with flour tortillas and lime wedges. Top with dairy sour cream, guacamole, salsa and pitted ripe olives as desired.

*1 package (1.27 ounces) Lawry's Spices & Seasonings for Fajitas, ¼ cup lime juice and ¼ cup vegetable oil can be substituted.

NEW–AGE REUBEN

A new twist on an old favorite.

½ medium head red cabbage,
  shredded
½ cup Lawry's Herb & Garlic
  Marinade with Lemon Juice

8 slices rye bread
¾ pound thinly sliced cooked
  turkey
¾ pound thinly sliced Swiss cheese

In large resealable plastic bag or bowl, combine cabbage and Herb & Garlic Marinade with Lemon Juice. Refrigerate at least 1 hour or overnight; drain. Layer ¼ of the cabbage mixture on top of each of four bread slices; top with turkey, cheese and remaining bread slices.

Makes 4 servings

PRESENTATION: To serve warm, wrap sandwiches in aluminum foil. Place in 300°F oven 20 minutes. Or, spread outside surfaces of bread with softened butter. Grill in nonstick skillet until browned on both sides.

HINT: Use turkey from the delicatessen.

Tex-Mex Chicken Fajitas

SPICY SESAME TURKEY SANDWICH

The entire family will enjoy this sandwich that has a touch of spice.

½ cup mayonnaise
1½ teaspoons Lawry's Pinch of
    Herbs, divided
1½ teaspoons Lawry's Lemon
    Pepper, divided
1 teaspoon sesame oil
1 teaspoon fresh lemon juice
4 or 5 turkey cutlets
    (about 1¼ pounds)

½ cup all-purpose flour
2 tablespoons toasted sesame
    seeds
¼ to ½ teaspoon cayenne pepper
¼ cup milk
¼ cup vegetable oil
6 whole wheat buns, toasted
1 tomato, cut into 6 slices
6 sprigs watercress

In small bowl, combine mayonnaise, ½ teaspoon Pinch of Herbs, ½ teaspoon
Lemon Pepper, sesame oil and lemon juice; cover. Refrigerate until ready to
serve. Cut turkey into six equal portions. In large resealable plastic bag,
combine flour, sesame seeds, cayenne pepper, remaining Pinch of Herbs and
remaining Lemon Pepper. Dip each turkey cutlet into milk. Add turkey, a
few pieces at a time, to plastic bag; seal bag. Shake until well coated. In large,
heavy skillet, heat oil over medium heat. Add turkey; cook 5 to 8 minutes or
until no longer pink in center, turning over after 3 minutes. Spread cut sides
of buns with mayonnaise mixture. Top bottom half of each bun with turkey;
cover with tomato, watercress and top half of roll.   *Makes 6 servings*

PRESENTATION: Serve with coleslaw and juicy watermelon.

LIME CILANTRO MARINATED CHICKEN

A fresh, light marinade for chicken.

4 boneless, skinless chicken breast
    halves (¾ to 1 pound)
1 cup finely chopped red onion
1 cup lime juice
½ cup red wine vinegar
½ cup chopped fresh cilantro
¼ cup vegetable oil

¼ cup frozen orange juice
    concentrate, thawed
1¾ teaspoons Lawry's Garlic Salt
1½ teaspoons Lawry's Seasoned
    Pepper
1 teaspoon chopped fresh mint

Pierce chicken several times with fork. Place in large resealable plastic bag or
shallow dish. In small bowl, combine remaining ingredients. Reserve 1 cup
seasoning mixture; pour remaining seasoning mixture over chicken. Seal bag
or cover dish. Refrigerate at least 45 minutes. Remove chicken from
marinade; discard marinade. Grill or broil, 4 to 5 inches from heat source,
10 to 12 minutes or until chicken is no longer pink in center, turning and
brushing occasionally with reserved 1 cup seasoning mixture.

Makes 4 servings

PRESENTATION: Serve with rice or warm tortillas and a green salad.

Right to left: Spicy Sesame Turkey
Sandwich, Coleslaw Supreme (page 68)

TURKEY TAMALE PIE WITH CORNBREAD

A complete meal that the whole family will enjoy, made with fresh turkey and ingredients from your pantry shelf.

2 tablespoons vegetable oil
1 small onion, chopped
1 small green bell pepper, chopped
1¼ pounds turkey cutlets, diced
1 can (15¼ ounces) whole kernel corn, drained
1 can (15 ounces) kidney beans, drained
1 can (14½ ounces) stewed tomatoes

1 can (6 ounces) tomato paste
½ cup water
1 package (1.25 ounces) Lawry's Taco Spices & Seasonings
1 can (4 ounces) diced green chiles, drained
1 package (16 ounces) cornbread mix

In large skillet, heat oil. Add onion and bell pepper; sauté 5 minutes. Add turkey; cook 7 to 10 minutes or until no longer pink in center, stirring occasionally. Reduce heat to low. Stir in corn, beans, stewed tomatoes, tomato paste, water, Taco Spices & Seasonings and green chiles. Simmer 10 minutes, stirring occasionally. Pour mixture into lightly greased 13×9-inch baking pan. In medium bowl, prepare cornbread batter according to package directions. Spoon dollops of batter over turkey mixture. Spoon remaining batter into lightly greased muffin tins. Bake in 375°F oven 25 minutes for casserole (15 to 20 minutes for muffins) or until toothpick inserted into cornbread comes out clean.   *Makes 8 to 10 servings*

PRESENTATION: Serve with a tossed green salad and your favorite cool beverage.

NOTE: Cool muffins completely. Wrap tightly and freeze for later use, if desired.

MESQUITE GRILLED CHICKEN EN CROÛTE

Grilled chicken wrapped in a cornbread biscuit.

4 boneless, skinless chicken breast halves (¾ to 1 pound)
¾ cup Lawry's Mesquite Marinade with Lime Juice
½ cup chopped red bell pepper
1 can (7 ounces) diced green chiles, drained
½ cup toasted pine nuts, finely chopped
¼ cup toasted walnuts, finely chopped (optional)

1 tablespoon lime juice
½ teaspoon Lawry's Seasoned Salt
½ teaspoon Lawry's Garlic Powder with Parsley
1 package (11 ounces) refrigerated cornstick dough *or* refrigerated breadstick dough
1 egg white, beaten

In large resealable plastic bag or shallow dish, place chicken. Add Mesquite Marinade with Lime Juice; seal bag or cover dish. Refrigerate at least 30 minutes or overnight. Grill or broil chicken, 4 to 5 inches from heat source, 7 to 10 minutes on each side or until no longer pink in center, turning over occasionally. Remove from grill; set aside. Heat oven to 350°F. In small bowl, combine bell pepper, chiles, nuts, lime juice, Seasoned Salt and Garlic Powder with Parsley. Roll dough out into four (8-inch) squares. On each square, place one chicken breast and equal portions of vegetable-nut mixture. Wrap dough around chicken and filling; seal edges of dough. Brush dough with egg white. Bake 3 to 5 minutes or until dough is golden brown and puffy. *Makes 4 servings*

PRESENTATION: Serve with a tossed green salad and fresh fruit.

CHICKEN WITH DILL SAUCE

If you enjoy the flavor of dill, you'll love this dish.

2 teaspoons vegetable oil	2 tablespoons Dijon-style mustard
4 boneless, skinless chicken breast halves (¾ to 1 pound)	½ teaspoon Lawry's Seasoned Pepper
2 green onions, sliced	¼ cup milk
½ teaspoon Lawry's Garlic Powder with Parsley	1½ teaspoons all-purpose flour
2 tablespoons water	2 tablespoons chopped fresh dill
	1 teaspoon lemon juice

In large nonstick skillet, heat oil. Add chicken; cook until browned on both sides. Remove chicken from skillet, reserving drippings in skillet; set chicken aside. In same skillet, sauté onion and Garlic Powder with Parsley. In small bowl, combine water, mustard and Seasoned Pepper; add to skillet. Return chicken to skillet. Bring to a boil. Reduce heat to low; cover. Simmer 10 to 12 minutes or until chicken is no longer pink in center. Remove chicken to serving plate; cover and keep warm. Reduce heat to low. In small bowl, slowly add milk to flour; blend well. Add to skillet. Cook just until thickened, stirring constantly. Remove from heat. Stir in dill and lemon juice.
Makes 4 servings

PRESENTATION: Spoon sauce over chicken. Serve with hot cooked rice and steamed fresh vegetables.

FISH & SEAFOOD

TERIYAKI SALMON STEAKS

Try this convenient way to serve salmon.

½ cup Lawry's Teriyaki Marinade
 with Pineapple Juice
¼ cup dry sherry
2 tablespoons orange juice

1 tablespoon Dijon-style mustard
4 salmon steaks (about 2 pounds)
1 large tomato, diced
½ cup thinly sliced green onion

In medium bowl, blend together Teriyaki Marinade with Pineapple Juice, sherry, orange juice and mustard with wire whisk. In large resealable plastic bag or shallow glass baking dish, place salmon; cover with marinade mixture. Seal bag or cover dish. Refrigerate at least 40 minutes, turning occasionally. In small bowl, combine tomato and green onion; set aside. Remove salmon from marinade, reserving marinade. Broil or grill, 4 inches from heat source, 3 to 5 minutes, brushing once with reserved marinade. Turn salmon over. Spoon vegetables over salmon; broil or grill 3 to 5 minutes longer or until thickest part of salmon flakes easily with fork. Garnish as desired.

Makes 4 servings

PRESENTATION: Delicious served with sautéed julienne potatoes or hot fluffy rice.

SEÑOR FISH

A deliciously different way to serve fish.

½ cup all-purpose flour
1 package (1.25 ounces) Lawry's
 Taco Spices & Seasonings
¾ teaspoon Lawry's Garlic Powder
 with Parsley
½ teaspoon Lawry's Seasoned
 Pepper

1 pound halibut *or* orange roughy
 fillets
2 tablespoons butter or margarine
 Lemon wedges

In shallow dish, combine flour, Taco Spices & Seasonings, Garlic Powder with Parsley and Seasoned Pepper. Rinse fish; pat dry with paper towels. Coat both sides of fish with flour mixture. In large nonstick skillet, melt butter. Add fish; cook 5 minutes on each side or until fish flakes easily with fork.

Makes 4 servings

PRESENTATION: Squeeze lemon wedges over fish when serving. Great with a rice and vegetable medley.

Teriyaki Salmon Steak

SPICY BROILED SHRIMP

A delicious combination of shrimp and seasonings.

¼ cup butter or margarine
2 tablespoons vegetable oil
1 bay leaf, crushed
2½ teaspoons Lawry's Seasoned Salt
¾ to 1 teaspoon hot pepper sauce
1 teaspoon dried rosemary, crushed

¾ teaspoon Lawry's Garlic Powder with Parsley
¼ teaspoon dried basil, crushed
¼ teaspoon dried oregano, crushed
1½ pounds large, fresh shrimp, peeled and deveined

In small saucepan, melt butter over low heat. Add all remaining ingredients except shrimp; cook, uncovered, 5 minutes. Rinse shrimp; pat dry with paper towels. Place on broiler pan. Brush generously with melted butter mixture. Broil, 5 inches from heat source, 5 minutes or until shrimp turn pink, turning and brushing frequently with melted butter mixture. Garnish as desired. *Makes 4 servings*

PRESENTATION: Spoon any remaining melted butter mixture over cooked shrimp. Serve with lemon wedges and warm bread. This recipe is also great served over hot cooked rice.

HINT: To prepare in skillet, heat butter mixture in skillet as directed above. Add shrimp; sauté 5 to 7 minutes or until shrimp turn pink. Serve as directed.

SEAFOOD DIJONNAISE

A perfect last-minute dinner idea.

1 pound salmon *or* halibut fillets
¾ cup Lawry's Dijon & Honey Barbecue Sauce
½ medium onion, sliced

¼ cup toasted slivered almonds
Chopped fresh parsley or watercress (garnish)
Lemon slices (garnish)

Place fish in shallow glass baking dish; cover with Dijon & Honey Barbecue Sauce. Top with onion slices and almonds; cover with aluminum foil. Bake in 350°F oven 20 minutes. Uncover; bake 5 minutes longer or until fish flakes easily with fork. *Makes 4 servings*

PRESENTATION: Garnish with chopped parsley and lemon slices.

CHICKEN DIJONNAISE: Substitute 1 pound boneless chicken breast halves for fish. Bake 25 to 30 minutes or until chicken is no longer pink in center.

Spicy Broiled Shrimp

TERIYAKI TROUT

Easy and quick.

4 whole trout (about 2 pounds)
¾ cup Lawry's Teriyaki Marinade
with Pineapple Juice
½ cup sliced green onion
2 medium lemons, sliced
Chopped fresh parsley (optional)

Pierce skin of trout several times with fork. Brush the inside and outside of each trout with Teriyaki Marinade with Pineapple Juice; stuff with green onion and lemon slices. Place in shallow glass baking dish. Pour all but ¼ cup Teriyaki Marinade with Pineapple Juice over trout; cover. Refrigerate at least 30 minutes. Meanwhile, heat grill. Remove trout from marinade, reserving marinade. Place trout in oiled grill basket; brush with reserved marinade. Grill, 4 to 5 inches from heat source, 10 minutes or until trout flakes easily with fork, turning and brushing occasionally with reserved ¼ cup Teriyaki Marinade with Pineapple Juice. Sprinkle with parsley, if desired.   *Makes 4 servings*

PRESENTATION: For a delicious side dish, cook sliced and oiled bell pepper, onion and zucchini on grill with trout.

CRAB CAKES

A delicious dish from the South.

1 egg
2 tablespoons mayonnaise
1 teaspoon dry mustard
1 teaspoon Lawry's Seasoned
Pepper
½ teaspoon Lawry's Seasoned Salt
¼ teaspoon cayenne pepper
4 cans (4¼ ounces *each*) crabmeat,
drained, rinsed and cartilage
removed
3 tablespoons finely chopped fresh
parsley
2 tablespoons soda cracker crumbs
Vegetable oil for frying
(about ½ cup)

In medium, deep bowl, beat egg. Blend in mayonnaise, mustard, Seasoned Pepper, Seasoned Salt and cayenne pepper. Add crabmeat, parsley and cracker crumbs; mix lightly. Divide mixture into eight equal portions; shape each into a ball, about 2 inches in diameter. Flatten each ball slightly; wrap in waxed paper. Refrigerate 30 minutes. In large, deep skillet, heat oil. Carefully add crab cakes, four at a time, to skillet. Fry 8 minutes or until golden brown on all sides, turning frequently. With slotted spoon, remove cakes from oil; drain on paper towels. Serve immediately.   *Makes 8 cakes*

PRESENTATION: Serve with tartar sauce and lemon wedges.

Teriyaki Trout

ENSENADA FISH TACOS

Fish tacos are a great way for kids to learn to love fish.

10 ounces halibut *or* orange roughy
 fillets, cut into 1-inch cubes
1 tablespoon vegetable oil
1 tablespoon lime juice
1 package (1.27 ounces) Lawry's
 Spices & Seasonings for
 Fajitas
6 corn *or* flour tortillas
 (approximately 8 inches
 round)
2½ cups shredded lettuce

½ cup diced tomatoes
¾ cup (3 ounces) shredded
 Monterey Jack *or* Cheddar
 cheese
2 tablespoons thinly sliced green
 onion
 Dairy sour cream (garnish)
 Guacamole (garnish)
 Salsa (garnish)
 Chopped fresh cilantro (garnish)

In shallow glass baking dish, place fish. Pour oil and lime juice over fish.
Sprinkle with Spices & Seasonings for Fajitas; toss lightly to coat. Cover.
Refrigerate 2 hours to marinate, occasionally spooning marinade over fish.
In same dish, bake fish in 450°F oven 10 minutes or until fish flakes easily
with fork; drain. To serve, evenly divide fish; place in center of each tortilla.
Top with lettuce, tomatoes, cheese and green onion.   *Makes 6 tacos*

PRESENTATION: Garnish each taco with sour cream, guacamole, salsa
and fresh cilantro, if desired.

ONION & MUSHROOM FISH FILLETS

An easy dish with a whole lot of flavor.

¼ cup olive oil
1 large onion, thinly sliced
1 teaspoon sugar
½ teaspoon paprika
1 to 1½ pounds snapper *or* halibut
 fillets
 Juice from 1 large lemon
1 teaspoon Lawry's Seasoned Salt

½ teaspoon Lawry's Lemon Pepper
6 ounces sliced fresh mushrooms
 (about 2 cups)
2 medium tomatoes, cut into thick
 slices
¼ cup dry sherry *or* vermouth
½ cup crushed seasoned croutons
 or crackers

In large skillet, heat oil. Add onion, sugar and paprika; sauté until onions are
tender and translucent. Spoon onion mixture into lightly greased 13×9-inch
baking dish. Rinse fish; pat dry with paper towels. Place on top of onions;
sprinkle with lemon juice, Seasoned Salt and Lemon Pepper. Top with
mushrooms and tomatoes; drizzle with sherry. Bake, uncovered, in 400°F
oven 10 minutes. Top with croutons; bake 10 minutes longer or until fish
flakes easily with fork.   *Makes 4 to 6 servings*

PRESENTATION: Serve with rice and fresh vegetables.

HINT: An ovenproof skillet can be used to eliminate use of baking dish.

Ensenada Fish Tacos

SERVE WITHS & MORE

If your salads and side dishes are singing the everyday blues, these innovative recipes featuring Lawry's Spice Blends and Classic Salad Dressings will help change their tune. Lawry's has created fresh new ways to make vegetables vivacious and salads superb.

SIDE & MAIN DISH SALADS

CHICKEN CAESAR SALAD

A Caesar salad made easy by using one of Lawry's expertly blended Caesar Dressings.

1 tablespoon *plus* 1½ teaspoons olive oil
4 boneless, skinless chicken breast halves (¾ to 1 pound), cut into strips
4 to 5 cups torn romaine lettuce (1 large head)
1 large Roma or 1 medium tomato, diced

½ cup grated fresh Parmesan cheese
1 bottle (8 ounces) Lawry's Creamy Caesar with Cracked Pepper Dressing *or* Lawry's Classic Caesar with Imported Anchovies Dressing
Seasoned croutons

In large skillet, heat oil. Add chicken. Sauté 7 to 10 minutes or until no longer pink in center, stirring frequently. In large salad bowl, combine lettuce, tomato, Parmesan cheese and chicken; mix lightly. Refrigerate. Before serving, add enough dressing to coat all ingredients; toss lightly. Sprinkle with croutons. *Makes 4 servings*

HINT: For extra flavor, grill chicken breast halves until no longer pink in center; slice thinly. Serve on salad.

Chicken Caesar Salad

MARINATED SUMMER SALAD

A light summer salad ideal for picnics.

4 medium zucchini, diced
1 can (8 ounces) garbanzo beans,
   drained
½ cup chopped red onion
1 medium tomato, diced

1 can (2¼ ounces) sliced pitted
   ripe olives, drained
¾ cup Lawry's Herb and Garlic
   Marinade with Lemon Juice

In large bowl, combine all ingredients; toss lightly. Cover. Refrigerate at least 30 minutes. Serve and garnish as desired. *Makes 4 servings*

PRESENTATION: Serve on lettuce-covered platter as a side dish with sandwiches or your favorite chicken recipe.

CREAMY PESTO SALAD DRESSING

A perfect dressing for any combination of greens or pasta.
Great as a vegetable dip, too!

½ cup packed fresh basil leaves,
   washed
2 tablespoons olive oil
1 tablespoon grated Parmesan
   cheese
1 teaspoon pine nuts (optional)
1½ teaspoons Lawry's Garlic
   Powder with Parsley

½ teaspoon Lawry's Seasoned Salt
1 cup mayonnaise
½ cup dairy sour cream
½ cup buttermilk
2 tablespoons red wine vinegar

Using food processor or blender, combine basil and oil until well blended. Add Parmesan cheese, pine nuts, Garlic Powder with Parsley and Seasoned Salt; process until smooth. Set aside. In small bowl, combine mayonnaise, sour cream and buttermilk with wire whisk. Add basil mixture and vinegar; blend until smooth. Refrigerate before serving. *Makes 2 cups*

PRESENTATION: Delicious over a salad of mixed romaine and iceberg lettuce, pitted ripe olives and slivered red bell peppers. Or, serve over a mixture of hot cooked rotini pasta, sliced green Spanish olives and slivered red bell peppers.

Marinated Summer Salad

TANGY GARLIC TORTELLINI SALAD

Garlic and pasta are the perfect combination.

¼ cup mayonnaise
¼ cup plain yogurt
1 tablespoon *plus* 1½ teaspoons
    lemon juice
1 tablespoon olive oil
2 teaspoons chopped fresh chives
    or ¼ cup chopped green onion
1 teaspoon Lawry's Seasoned
    Pepper
1 to 1¼ teaspoons Lawry's Garlic
    Salt

9 ounces fresh cheese-filled
    tortellini *or* 8 ounces spiral
    pasta, cooked and drained
1 medium-sized red bell pepper,
    cut into thin strips
1 medium zucchini, cut into
    julienne strips
2 medium carrots, cut into julienne
    strips

In small bowl, combine all ingredients except pasta and vegetables. In medium bowl, combine pasta and vegetables; mix lightly. Add dressing; toss lightly to coat. Refrigerate at least 30 minutes. Garnish as desired.

Makes 4 to 6 servings

PRESENTATION: Serve with crusty French or sourdough bread.

CAESAR SALAD REFRESHER

These unique ingredients give everyday salads a refreshing change.

7 cups torn romaine lettuce
1 jar (14 ounces) hearts of palm,
    drained and cut into 1½-inch
    julienne strips
2 bunches watercress, well
    trimmed

1 bunch radishes, thinly sliced
1 shallot, minced
1 bottle (8 ounces) Lawry's Classic
    Caesar with Imported
    Anchovies Dressing, chilled

In medium bowl, combine lettuce, hearts of palm, watercress, radishes and shallot; refrigerate. Add dressing just before serving; toss lightly to coat.

Makes 6 servings

PRESENTATION: Serve on large platter to show off ingredients.

Tangy Garlic Tortellini Salad

MEDITERRANEAN GREEK SALAD

This popular Greek salad is now easy to prepare in your own kitchen.

½ cup olive oil
⅓ cup red wine vinegar
2 teaspoons chopped fresh oregano
or ¾ teaspoon dried oregano
1 teaspoon Lawry's Seasoned Salt
1 teaspoon Lawry's Garlic Powder
with Parsley
3 medium cucumbers, peeled and
chopped

3 to 4 medium tomatoes, cored and
coarsely chopped
1 medium onion, thinly sliced and
separated into rings
1 can (6 ounces) Greek olives,
pitted, or 1 can (6 ounces)
pitted ripe olives, drained
1 cup (4 ounces) crumbled feta
cheese

In container with stopper or lid, combine oil, vinegar, oregano and
seasonings; cover and shake well. Set dressing aside. In medium bowl,
combine cucumbers, tomatoes, onion, olives and cheese; mix lightly. Shake
dressing. Add to salad; toss lightly to coat. Refrigerate 30 minutes.

Makes 8 servings

PRESENTATION: Serve with a slotted spoon on lettuce-covered platter, if
desired. Crusty rolls or warm pita bread are a perfect accompaniment.

VARIATION: Add dressing to 2 cups torn romaine lettuce instead of
vegetable mixture.

HEALTHY CARROT SALAD

A light-style dressing brings a new flavor to this favorite salad.

4 cups shredded carrots
¼ cup raisins
¼ cup chopped walnuts
½ cup orange juice

¼ cup plain yogurt
1 tablespoon vegetable oil
¾ teaspoon Lawry's Seasoned Salt
½ teaspoon Lawry's Lemon Pepper

In medium bowl, combine carrots, raisins and walnuts. In container with
stopper or lid, combine remaining ingredients; cover and shake well. Add to
carrot mixture; mix lightly to coat. *Makes 6 servings*

PRESENTATION: A cool side-dish salad for sandwiches or a terrific salad
to serve on a picnic.

Mediterranean Greek Salad

SOUTHWESTERN CHICKEN SALAD

Perfect served just with warm, fresh bread.

1 package (1.27 ounces) Lawry's Spices & Seasonings for Fajitas
3 tablespoons vegetable oil
2 tablespoons *plus* 1½ teaspoons lime juice
1½ teaspoons Lawry's Garlic Powder with Parsley
6 boneless, skinless chicken breast halves (about 1½ pounds)

6 cups torn lettuce
½ medium-sized red onion, thinly sliced
1 large tomato, cut into wedges
1 can (2¼ ounces) sliced pitted ripe olives, drained
1 avocado, peeled, pitted and thinly sliced
Ranch dressing

In small bowl, combine Spices & Seasonings for Fajitas, oil, lime juice and Garlic Powder with Parsley. Pierce chicken several times with fork. Place chicken in large resealable plastic bag or shallow glass baking dish. Add seasoning mixture; seal bag or cover dish. Marinate in refrigerator at least 30 minutes or overnight, turning occasionally. Remove chicken from marinade. Grill or broil, 4 to 5 inches from heat source, 7 to 10 minutes on each side or until chicken is no longer pink in center. Cool slightly. Cut chicken into thin slices or cubes. To arrange individual salads, cover salad plates with lettuce; top with chicken, onion, tomatoes, olives and avocado.

Makes 4 to 6 servings

PRESENTATION: Drizzle with ranch dressing.

MUSHROOM ARTICHOKE SALAD

A refreshing and tasty combination.

2 cans (14 ounces *each*) water-packed artichoke hearts, drained and quartered
1 pound fresh mushrooms, sliced

2 cups cherry tomatoes, cut into halves
½ cup Lawry's Herb & Garlic Marinade with Lemon Juice

In large glass bowl or resealable plastic bag, combine artichokes, mushrooms and tomatoes; mix lightly. Add Herb & Garlic Marinade with Lemon Juice; stir or seal bag and toss lightly to coat. Refrigerate at least 1 hour.

Makes 6 servings

PRESENTATION: Serve as an appetizer or side dish.

NOTE: Flavors are best if salad is refrigerated overnight.

Southwestern Chicken Salad

PRIDE OF THE CROWNS' SALAD

As served at Lawry's The Five Crowns restaurant in Corona del Mar.

1 teaspoon dry mustard
1 teaspoon Lawry's Seasoned Salt
1 teaspoon Lawry's Seasoned
  Pepper
1 teaspoon Lawry's Pinch of
  Herbs
¼ teaspoon Lawry's Garlic Powder
  with Parsley
½ cup red wine vinegar

¾ cup olive oil
2 heads Bibb lettuce, torn into
  bite-size pieces
½ to ¾ cup chopped walnuts
¼ pound bacon, diced, cooked and
  drained
½ cup (2 ounces) coarsely shredded
  Gruyère cheese
1½ cups seasoned croutons

In container with stopper or lid, combine mustard, seasonings and vinegar; cover and shake well. Add olive oil; cover and shake until blended. Refrigerate several hours to blend flavors. In large salad bowl, combine remaining ingredients. Shake dressing. Add to salad; toss lightly to coat.

Makes 6 servings

PRESENTATION: Serve on chilled salad plates with a chilled salad fork.

PIZZA SALAD

A fresh salad with the ingredients of a pizza.

3 cups torn lettuce
3 small tomatoes, sliced
2 cups (8 ounces) shredded
  mozzarella cheese
6 ounces fresh mushrooms, sliced
2 ounces thinly sliced pepperoni
½ cup chopped green bell pepper
½ teaspoon Lawry's Garlic Powder
  with Parsley

½ teaspoon Lawry's Seasoned
  Pepper
½ to ¾ cup Lawry's Classic Italian
  with Aged Parmesan Cheese
  Dressing
1 cup croutons

In large salad bowl, place lettuce, tomatoes, cheese, mushrooms, pepperoni, bell pepper, Garlic Powder with Parsley and Seasoned Pepper; mix lightly. Add dressing; toss to coat. Refrigerate at least 30 minutes. Sprinkle with croutons just before serving.

Makes 4 servings

PRESENTATION: Serve with fresh bread and iced tea.

Pride of the Crowns' Salad

TOMATO BASIL PASTA

A trendy way to serve pasta.

½ cup vegetable oil, divided
¼ cup olive oil
1 teaspoon mustard powder
3 tablespoons balsamic vinegar
2 tablespoons red wine vinegar
2 teaspoons Lawry's Garlic
  Powder with Parsley
2 teaspoons Lawry's Lemon
  Pepper
1½ teaspoons Lawry's Seasoned
  Salt
¼ cup marinated sun-dried
  tomatoes, drained and
  chopped

2 tablespoons chopped fresh basil
4 boneless, skinless chicken breast
  halves (¾ to 1 pound), cut into
  thin strips
1 medium zucchini, cut into
  julienne strips
1 can (2¼ ounces) pitted ripe
  olives, drained
8 ounces penne pasta, cooked,
  drained and kept hot
  Chopped fresh parsley (optional)

In medium bowl, blend ⅓ cup vegetable oil, olive oil, mustard powder and
vinegars with wire whisk. Stir in Garlic Powder with Parsley, Lemon Pepper,
Seasoned Salt, sun-dried tomatoes and basil. Refrigerate. In large, deep
skillet, heat remaining vegetable oil. Add chicken; sauté 7 to 10 minutes or
until no longer pink in center, stirring occasionally. Remove chicken from
skillet; set aside. Add zucchini and olives to skillet; sauté 5 minutes or until
zucchini is crisp-tender. Return chicken to skillet along with hot pasta and
enough prepared dressing to coat; toss lightly. Serve with any remaining
dressing. *Makes 4 to 6 servings*

PRESENTATION: Sprinkle with chopped fresh parsley, if desired.

HINT: Processing dressing in food processor or blender for 1 minute will
make a smoother dressing.

COLESLAW SUPREME

A touch of sweetness and zing!

4 cups shredded green cabbage
2 cups shredded red cabbage
⅓ cup chopped green onion
½ cup sliced celery
¼ cup chopped peanuts

1 can (8 ounces) sliced peaches,
  drained and chopped
½ teaspoon Lawry's Garlic Salt
¼ cup French dressing
¼ teaspoon celery seed

In large bowl, combine all ingredients; mix well. Refrigerate at least 30
minutes. *Makes 4 to 6 servings*

PRESENTATION: Serve with sandwiches and barbecued foods.

VARIATION: Substitute 1 package (8 ounces) preshredded coleslaw mix for
the 6 cups shredded cabbage.

MEXICAN–STYLE DRESSINGS

Three unique dressings each with their own touch of Mexico.

MEXICAN VINAIGRETTE DRESSING

1 cup vegetable oil
1 teaspoon mustard powder
¼ cup lime juice
2 tablespoons white wine vinegar
1 package (1.25 ounces) Lawry's
  Taco Spices & Seasonings

⅓ cup diced roasted red peppers
1 teaspoon Lawry's Garlic Powder
  with Parsley
1 teaspoon dried oregano
1 teaspoon dried cilantro

In medium bowl, blend oil, mustard powder, lime juice and vinegar with wire whisk. Add remaining ingredients; blend well. Refrigerate until ready to use. *Makes 1½ cups*

PRESENTATION: Serve over mixed salad greens or a colorful mixture of steamed broccoli, corn, tomatoes and cucumbers.

HINT: Processing final mixture in food processor or blender for 1 minute will make a smoother dressing.

CREAMY MEXICAN DRESSING

1 cup mayonnaise
½ cup dairy sour cream
½ cup buttermilk
1 package (1.25 ounces) Lawry's
  Taco Spices & Seasonings

1 teaspoon Lawry's Garlic Pepper
1 teaspoon dried oregano
1 teaspoon dried cilantro
2 tablespoons lime juice

In medium bowl, blend mayonnaise, sour cream and buttermilk with wire whisk. Blend in Taco Spices & Seasonings, Garlic Pepper, oregano, cilantro and lime juice. Refrigerate until ready to use. *Makes 2 cups*

PRESENTATION: Serve over any combination of torn iceberg, romaine or spinach. Or, serve as a zesty dip.

SPICY MEXICAN DRESSING

¾ cup Italian dressing
2 teaspoons chopped fresh cilantro
½ to ¾ teaspoon hot pepper sauce

½ teaspoon Lawry's Seasoned
  Pepper
½ teaspoon chili powder

In medium bowl, combine all ingredients; blend well. *Makes 3 cups*

PRESENTATION: Serve dressing with California Black Bean Salad (page 80) or over tossed greens for a spicy salad dressing variation.

VEGETABLES, BEANS & RICE

MARINATED TOMATOES & MOZZARELLA

An attractive, succulent way to serve tomatoes.

1 medium bunch fresh basil leaves,
  divided
1 pound Italian tomatoes, sliced
½ pound fresh packed buffalo
  mozzarella cheese, sliced
¼ cup olive oil
3 tablespoons chopped fresh
  chives

2 tablespoons red wine vinegar
2 teaspoons sugar
½ teaspoon dried oregano
½ teaspoon Lawry's Seasoned
  Pepper
½ teaspoon Lawry's Garlic Powder
  with Parsley

Divide basil in half; reserve one half for garnish. Chop remaining basil leaves; set aside. In shallow dish, place tomato slices and cheese. Combine all remaining ingredients except reserved whole or chopped basil leaves; pour over tomatoes and cheese. Cover. Refrigerate at least 30 minutes. To serve, arrange tomato and cheese slices on serving plate. Sprinkle with chopped basil leaves. Garnish with reserved whole basil leaves.

Makes 4 to 6 servings

PRESENTATION: Serve with grilled chicken sandwiches or as a zesty Italian appetizer.

CALIFORNIA MARINATED MUSHROOMS

The longer these marinate, the tastier they are.

1 pound small fresh mushrooms,
  cleaned
1 small cucumber, peeled and
  sliced
1 jar (4 ounces) chopped pimiento,
  drained

1 bottle (8 ounces) Lawry's Classic
  Red Wine Vinaigrette with
  Cabernet Sauvignon Dressing
½ teaspoon Lawry's Garlic Salt

In large resealable plastic bag or medium glass bowl, combine all ingredients; seal bag or cover dish. Refrigerate at least 1 hour, turning bag over or stirring occasionally. *Makes 8 appetizer servings*

PRESENTATION: Serve in lettuce cup made with layers of curly lettuce, red cabbage and radicchio.

Marinated Tomatoes & Mozzarella

SANTA FE POTATO CAKES

A delicious, unique way to enjoy potatoes.

3 cups *cooked* instant mashed
   potato flakes or leftover
   unbuttered mashed potatoes
1 can (4 ounces) diced green chiles,
   drained
²/₃ cup cornmeal, divided
3 green onions, sliced
¹/₃ cup (about 1½ ounces) shredded
   Cheddar cheese
2 eggs, beaten

2 tablespoons chopped fresh
   cilantro
1 teaspoon chili powder
½ teaspoon Lawry's Seasoned Salt
½ teaspoon Lawry's Seasoned
   Pepper
2 tablespoons olive oil, divided
   Salsa
   Dairy sour cream

In large bowl, combine potatoes, chiles, ½ cup cornmeal, onion, cheese, eggs, cilantro, chili powder, Seasoned Salt and Seasoned Pepper; shape into eight patties. Sprinkle both sides with remaining cornmeal; set aside. In large nonstick skillet, heat 1 tablespoon oil over medium heat. Add four patties; cook 5 to 7 minutes or until golden brown, turning once. Remove from skillet; keep warm. Repeat with remaining oil and patties. Garnish as desired.   *Makes 4 servings*

PRESENTATION: Serve with salsa and sour cream.

HERBED WILD RICE

The perfect side dish to chicken, turkey or pork chops.

1 tablespoon margarine or butter
3 cups sliced fresh mushrooms
1 cup uncooked wild rice blend
¾ cup chopped onion
1 can (14½ ounces) chicken broth
½ cup water
1 medium tomato, diced

1 teaspoon dried basil
1 teaspoon dried oregano
1 teaspoon Lawry's Lemon Pepper
¾ teaspoon Lawry's Garlic Powder
   with Parsley
½ teaspoon Lawry's Seasoned Salt

In large saucepan, melt margarine. Add mushrooms, rice and onion; sauté 5 minutes. Stir in remaining ingredients. Bring to a boil. Reduce heat to low; cover. Simmer 30 minutes or until liquid is absorbed and rice is tender.
                                                        Makes 6 servings

PRESENTATION: For extra color, sprinkle finished dish with chopped fresh parsley, if desired.

Santa Fe Potato Cakes

BROCCOLI WITH SESAME VINAIGRETTE

Microwaved vegetables are easy and keep their bright color.

1 teaspoon butter or margarine
1 teaspoon sesame seeds
1 pound fresh broccoli
2 tablespoons *plus* 1½ teaspoons
　white wine vinegar

1 tablespoon water
2 teaspoons olive or sesame oil
½ teaspoon Lawry's Seasoned Salt
½ teaspoon Lawry's Seasoned
　Pepper

MICROWAVE DIRECTIONS: On shallow microwave-safe plate, place butter and sesame seeds. Cover with plastic wrap. Microwave on HIGH 1 minute or until seeds are toasted; set aside. Trim off large ends of lower broccoli stalks; discard. Place trimmed broccoli in shallow microwave-safe dish; cover. Microwave on HIGH 7 minutes or until broccoli is crisp-tender. Place broccoli on serving platter; keep warm. Combine sesame seeds, vinegar, water, oil, Seasoned Salt and Seasoned Pepper; drizzle over broccoli. Garnish as desired. *Makes 4 servings*

PRESENTATION: Serve with any grilled meat or poultry.

MARSHMALLOW SWEET POTATO BAKE

A festive dish with mouth-watering flavor.

5 or 6 medium-sized sweet
　potatoes
½ cup chopped pecans
⅓ cup packed brown sugar
1 tablespoon frozen orange juice
　concentrate, thawed
½ teaspoon Lawry's Seasoned Salt

¼ teaspoon ground cinnamon
¼ teaspoon ground nutmeg
2 tablespoons butter or margarine,
　cut into pieces
1 to 1½ cups miniature
　marshmallows

In medium saucepan, cook potatoes in boiling water until tender; cool. Peel potatoes. Place in medium bowl; mash well. Add pecans, brown sugar, orange juice concentrate, Seasoned Salt, cinnamon and nutmeg; blend well. In lightly greased 9-inch square glass baking dish, place potato mixture. Top with butter pieces. Bake in 300°F oven 20 minutes. Sprinkle with marshmallows. Place under broiler; broil just until marshmallows are lightly toasted. *Makes 6 servings*

PRESENTATION: Perfect with any entrée.

VARIATION: Substitute canned yams for fresh sweet potatoes.

Broccoli with Sesame Vinaigrette

GARLIC SKILLET POTATOES

A great alternative to a plain baked potato.

2 tablespoons vegetable or olive oil
4 large red-skinned potatoes, cut
   into thin wedges
½ cup chopped onion
1¼ teaspoons Lawry's Garlic
   Powder with Parsley

¾ to 1 teaspoon Lawry's Seasoned
   Salt
¾ teaspoon Lawry's Seasoned
   Pepper
½ teaspoon sugar
   Chopped fresh parsley (garnish)

In large skillet, heat oil over medium heat. Add potatoes, onion, Garlic
Powder with Parsley, Seasoned Salt, Seasoned Pepper and sugar. Cook,
uncovered, over medium heat 25 to 30 minutes or until potatoes are tender
and browned.   *Makes 4 to 6 servings*

PRESENTATION: Sprinkle with chopped parsley. Great served with steak,
baked chicken, scrambled eggs or omelets.

SPICY GREEN BEAN SAUTÉ

Give your side dish an Oriental flavor.

2 tablespoons vegetable oil
1 pound fresh green beans,
   trimmed
½ cup diced red bell pepper
1 medium onion, sliced
2 teaspoons minced fresh ginger
1 teaspoon Lawry's Garlic Powder
   with Parsley

¾ cup chicken broth
½ cup Lawry's Teriyaki Marinade
   with Pineapple Juice
2 teaspoons cornstarch
¼ teaspoon cayenne pepper
   (optional)

In large skillet, heat oil. Add green beans, bell pepper, onion, ginger and
Garlic Powder with Parsley; sauté 5 minutes or until vegetables are crisp-
tender. In small bowl, combine broth, Teriyaki Marinade with Pineapple
Juice, cornstarch and cayenne pepper. Add to vegetable mixture; continue
cooking until sauce is thick and clear, stirring constantly.
                                                    Makes 4 to 6 servings

PRESENTATION: Serve with thinly sliced beef or baked chicken.

Garlic Skillet Potatoes

CHEESY CORN BAKE

A great change of pace from plain cornbread.

3 eggs, well beaten
1 can (16 ounces) creamed corn
¾ cup unseasoned dry bread
  crumbs
¾ cup (3 ounces) shredded
  Cheddar cheese
½ cup hot milk
½ medium-sized green bell pepper,
  chopped

3 teaspoons chopped onion
1 teaspoon Lawry's Seasoned Salt
¾ teaspoon Lawry's Seasoned
  Pepper
¼ teaspoon Lawry's Garlic Powder
  with Parsley

Preheat oven to 350°F. In large bowl, combine all ingredients. Pour into
ungreased 2-quart casserole. Bake in 350°F oven 1 hour. Let stand 10
minutes before serving.   *Makes 6 servings*

PRESENTATION: Serve with meat loaf, baked chicken or fried fish.

HINT: Serve topped with prepared Lawry's Original Style Spaghetti Sauce
for extra flavor.

SWEET GLAZED CARROTS

Carrots become extra-special when prepared this way.

1 pound fresh whole baby carrots,
  peeled
¼ cup water

⅓ cup orange marmalade
1 tablespoon butter or margarine
1 teaspoon Lawry's Seasoned Salt

In 1½-quart microwave-safe casserole, place carrots and water. Cover with
plastic wrap; vent one corner. Microwave on HIGH 7 to 8 minutes or until
carrots are tender, stirring after 5 minutes; drain. Immediately stir in
remaining ingredients.   *Makes 4 to 5 servings*

PRESENTATION: Serve with broiled or grilled fish, poultry or beef.

CONVENTIONAL DIRECTIONS: In medium saucepan, place ½ cup
water. Set vegetable steamer in pan; bring water to a boil. Place carrots in
steamer; cover pan. Steam carrots 10 minutes or until tender. Remove
carrots to serving bowl. Immediately stir in remaining ingredients.

VARIATION: Substitute 1 package (16 ounces) frozen crinkle-cut carrots or
1 pound fresh carrots, thinly sliced, for baby carrots.

Cheesy Corn Bake

SPICY CHEESE BROCCOLI

A simple recipe for everyday meals.

5 cups broccoli florets
5 ounces pasteurized process
   American cheese spread,
   cubed
¾ cup (3 ounces) shredded mild
   Cheddar cheese

⅔ cup Lawry's Chunky Taco Sauce
   or chunky medium salsa
¼ cup sliced green onion
½ teaspoon Lawry's Garlic Powder
   with Parsley

MICROWAVE DIRECTIONS: In large microwave-safe bowl, place
broccoli; cover with plastic wrap. Microwave on HIGH 10 minutes; set aside.
In medium microwave-safe bowl, combine remaining ingredients.
Microwave on HIGH 2 to 3 minutes or until smooth, stirring after each
minute.   *Makes 4 servings*

PRESENTATION: Drain vegetables; place on serving platter. Top with
cheese sauce.

PARMESANO ZUCCHINI

The perfect Italian side dish.

2 tablespoons olive oil
2 medium zucchini, cut into
   julienne strips
1 small red onion, thinly sliced
6 ounces sliced fresh mushrooms
   (about 2 cups)

¼ cup chopped fresh basil leaves
½ teaspoon Lawry's Garlic Powder
   with Parsley
½ teaspoon Lawry's Seasoned Salt
⅓ cup freshly grated Parmesan
   cheese

In medium skillet, heat oil. Add all remaining ingredients except cheese;
sauté 3 minutes or until zucchini is tender.   *Makes 4 servings*

PRESENTATION: Sprinkle with Parmesan cheese just before serving.

CALIFORNIA BLACK BEAN SALAD

A spicy-hot dressing makes this salad a trendy favorite.

1 can (15 ounces) black beans,
   drained and rinsed
1 can (12 ounces) whole kernel
   corn, drained
1 medium tomato, chopped
½ cup chopped red onion

½ cup chopped green bell pepper
½ teaspoon Lawry's Garlic Powder
   with Parsley
Spicy Mexican Dressing
   (page 69)

In large bowl, combine all ingredients except Spicy Mexican Dressing; blend well. Add dressing; toss to coat. Refrigerate at least 15 minutes.

Makes 6 servings

PRESENTATION: Serve with your favorite Mexican recipe.

MEXICALI RICE AND BEANS

Lots of extras to make rice special.

1 can (14½ ounces) chicken broth
1 can (4 ounces) diced green chiles, drained
1 package (1.25 ounces) Lawry's Mexican Rice Spices & Seasonings
¾ teaspoon Lawry's Garlic Powder with Parsley
½ teaspoon lemon juice
¾ cup uncooked long-grain rice
1 can (15 ounces) pinto beans, drained
1 medium tomato, chopped
1 medium avocado, peeled, pitted and chopped
1 teaspoon chopped fresh cilantro

In medium saucepan, combine all ingredients except beans, tomato, avocado and cilantro. Bring to a boil. Reduce heat to low; simmer, uncovered, 20 minutes or until rice is tender, stirring occasionally. Stir in remaining ingredients; simmer 5 minutes.

Makes 4 servings

PRESENTATION: Serve with soft tacos. Garnish with a sprig of fresh cilantro, if desired.

ROASTED SAVORY POTATOES

Simple to prepare and big on flavor.

½ cup mayonnaise*
1 teaspoon Lawry's Garlic Powder with Parsley
½ to ¾ teaspoon Lawry's Seasoned Pepper
½ teaspoon Lawry's Seasoned Salt
¼ teaspoon dried rosemary, crushed (optional)
2 medium russet potatoes, cut into ¼-inch-thick slices
½ cup sliced green onion
¼ cup (1 ounce) grated Parmesan cheese

In 9-inch square glass baking dish, combine mayonnaise, seasonings and rosemary. Add potatoes and onion; stir gently to coat. Sprinkle with cheese. Cover. Bake in 350°F oven 45 minutes; uncover. Bake 5 minutes longer to brown.

Makes 4 to 6 servings

PRESENTATION: Serve with grilled meat, fish or poultry.

HINT: For a hint of mustard try this idea: Reduce mayonnaise to ¼ cup and add ¼ cup Dijon-style mustard. Continue as directed.

*Reduced calorie mayonnaise works great too!

ALL THE REST

Look to this chapter when you're in the mood for pasta, breads, sandwiches and soups seasoned to perfection. Whether it's an Oriental, Italian or South-of-the border flavor you crave, Lawry's full line of flavorful seasonings deliver world-class fare to your table with ease.

PASTAS, ETC.

SPICY THAI NOODLES

Add cooked shredded chicken or sautéed shrimp for a main dish.

1¼ cups water
2½ teaspoons brown sugar
2 teaspoons soy sauce
1 teaspoon Lawry's Garlic Powder with Parsley
¾ teaspoon Lawry's Seasoned Salt
½ teaspoon cornstarch
⅛ to ¼ teaspoon hot pepper flakes

¼ cup chunky peanut butter
¼ cup sliced green onion
1 tablespoon chopped fresh cilantro
8 ounces linguine, cooked, drained and kept hot
1½ cups shredded red cabbage

In large, deep skillet, combine first seven ingredients. Bring to a boil. Reduce heat to low; simmer, uncovered, 5 minutes. Cool 10 minutes. Stir in peanut butter, green onion and cilantro. Add hot linguine and cabbage; toss lightly to coat. Serve immediately. Garnish as desired. *Makes 4 servings*

PRESENTATION: Great served with a marinated cucumber salad.

HINT: For a main dish, sauté ¾ pound peeled and deveined shrimp in skillet with 2 tablespoons butter and ½ teaspoon Lawry's Garlic Powder with Parsley. Add to hot linguine mixture; toss lightly.

Spicy Thai Noodles

SPICY EMPANADAS

Empanadas are tasty little hand-held treats.

1 can (8¾ ounces) garbanzo beans, drained
1 teaspoon vegetable oil
¼ cup minced fresh onion
2 tablespoons minced green bell pepper
¼ teaspoon Lawry's Garlic Powder with Parsley
2 tablespoons currants
2 tablespoons chopped pitted ripe olives

1 package (1.25 ounces) Lawry's Taco Spices & Seasonings
1 teaspoon lemon juice
¼ cup (1 ounce) shredded Monterey Jack cheese
All-purpose flour
1 sheet frozen puff pastry, thawed
1 egg yolk, beaten

Preheat oven to 400°F. In food processor or blender, place garbanzo beans. Pulse 30 seconds to chop finely; set aside. In large skillet, heat oil. Add onion, bell pepper and Garlic Powder with Parsley; sauté 3 to 4 minutes or until vegetables are crisp-tender. Add beans, currants, olives, Taco Spices & Seasonings and lemon juice; cook until mixture thickens, stirring occasionally. Remove from heat; stir in cheese. On lightly floured surface, roll out pastry sheet to approximately 18×10-inch rectangle; cut out six to eight (4-inch) circles. Spoon equal amounts of filling onto half of each circle; fold pastry over to form half circle. Press edges together with fork to seal. Place empañadas on greased baking sheet; brush with egg yolk. Bake 18 to 20 minutes or until golden brown. Garnish as desired.

Makes 6 to 8 empanadas

PRESENTATION: Great with salsa, dairy sour cream and peeled avocado slices.

HINT: Double recipe for more appetizers

GARLIC PARMESAN PASTA

Quick and convenient to prepare with a robust flavor.

⅓ cup butter or margarine
2 teaspoons dried basil, crushed
2 teaspoons lemon juice
1¼ teaspoons Lawry's Garlic Powder with Parsley
¾ teaspoon Lawry's Seasoned Salt
8 ounces fettuccine noodles, cooked, drained and kept hot

1½ cups broccoli florets, cooked crisp-tender
3 tablespoons chopped walnuts
½ cup grated Parmesan *or* Romano cheese

In large skillet, melt butter with basil, lemon juice, Garlic Powder with Parsley and Seasoned Salt. Add hot fettuccine, broccoli and walnuts; toss lightly to coat. Add cheese; toss to coat.

Makes 4 servings

PRESENTATION: Fresh fruit or sherbet for dessert adds a light touch.

MEATLESS MUFFALETTA SANDWICH

A trendy sandwich idea.

1 (12-inch) loaf French- or Italian-
style bread, unsliced
½ cup Lawry's Classic Red Wine
Vinaigrette with Cabernet
Sauvignon Dressing
½ cup mayonnaise
2 teaspoons capers
1 ripe avocado, peeled, pitted and
sliced
½ cup sliced green Spanish olives

1 can (2¼ ounces) sliced pitted
ripe olives, drained
4 ounces sliced Swiss cheese
Fresh basil leaves
4 Roma tomatoes, sliced, *or*
4 ounces roasted red pepper
slices
3 thin slices red onion, separated
into rings

Slice bread horizontally. Hollow out each loaf, leaving ¾-inch shell. (Tear removed bread into crumbs; freeze for another use.) Set bread shells aside. In food processor or blender, place Classic Red Wine Vinaigrette with Cabernet Sauvignon Dressing, mayonnaise and capers; process until well blended. Spread vinaigrette mixture evenly onto insides of shells. Into bottom bread shell, evenly layer remaining ingredients. Cover with top half of bread; press bread halves together firmly. Wrap tightly in plastic wrap; refrigerate 30 minutes. *Makes 4 servings*

PRESENTATION: Unwrap loaf; slice into four (3-inch) portions. Flavors are best when sandwich is served at room temperature. For crispier crust, place *uncut* loaf in 225°F oven. Bake 15 to 20 minutes. Remove from oven. Cut and fill loaf as directed.

NOTE: If desired, rinse olives in cold water to reduce saltiness.

ORIENTAL NOODLES

A great pasta side dish.

1 tablespoon *plus* 1½ teaspoons
vegetable oil
1 small green bell pepper, thinly
sliced
1 small red bell pepper, thinly
sliced
2 tablespoons soy sauce
2 teaspoons sesame oil

1 teaspoon brown sugar
½ teaspoon ground ginger
½ teaspoon Lawry's Garlic Powder
with Parsley
½ teaspoon Lawry's Seasoned
Pepper
6 ounces spaghetti or vermicelli,
cooked, drained and kept hot

In large skillet, heat vegetable oil. Add bell peppers; sauté until crisp-tender. Stir in soy sauce, sesame oil, brown sugar, ginger, Garlic Powder with Parsley and Seasoned Pepper. Add hot spaghetti; toss lightly to coat.
Makes 6 servings

PRESENTATION: Serve with grilled poultry or meat.

Meatless Muffaletta Sandwiches

CHINESE FLATBREADS

Reminiscent of the pan-fried scallion breads sold on the streets of Central China, this baked version is easier to make.

1 (1-pound) frozen white bread
    loaf, thawed
All-purpose flour
Sesame oil

2 teaspoons Lawry's Garlic Salt
⅓ cup thinly sliced green onion
2 teaspoons sesame seeds

Preheat oven to 400°F. Cut dough into eight equal pieces. On lightly floured work surface, roll each piece between palms of hands to form oblong shape. With rolling pin, roll one piece into 8×4-inch rectangle; brush lightly with sesame oil. Sprinkle with ¼ teaspoon Garlic Salt and ⅛ of the green onion. Starting from long side, roll up dough, jelly-roll fashion. With seam side down, shape dough into coil, stretching dough slightly as you go; tuck in ends to seal. Flatten coil slightly by pressing with heel of hand; roll out to 5-inch circle with rolling pin. Place coil on lightly greased baking sheet. Repeat with remaining dough. Brush tops lightly with sesame oil; sprinkle with sesame seeds. Bake 15 minutes or until golden brown.   *Makes 8 flatbreads*

PRESENTATION: Serve as an accompaniment to an Oriental chicken salad or as an appetizer for company.

HINT: Breads can be baked ahead, then frozen. Thaw and reheat in 350°F oven 5 minutes.

PESTO PASTA

A simple meal; a nice change from red sauce.

1½ cups fresh basil leaves
½ cup shelled walnuts
1½ teaspoons Lawry's Garlic
    Powder with Parsley
½ cup olive oil
½ cup grated fresh Parmesan
    cheese

¾ teaspoon Lawry's Seasoned Salt
¾ teaspoon Lawry's Seasoned
    Pepper
8 ounces spaghetti, cooked,
    drained and kept hot

In food processor or blender, place basil, walnuts and Garlic Powder with Parsley. Pulse until well blended. Slowly add oil; pulse until well blended. Add cheese, Seasoned Salt and Seasoned Pepper; pulse 1 minute. Place pesto in small saucepan; bring just to a boil over low heat. Combine pesto with hot spaghetti; toss lightly to coat.   *Makes 6 servings*

PRESENTATION: Top with grated fresh Parmesan cheese. Serve with French bread.

Chinese Flatbreads

SANTA FE TACO STEW

A very easy stew when "plain old regular" won't do.
This one has a spicy kick to it.

1 tablespoon vegetable oil
½ cup diced onion
½ teaspoon Lawry's Garlic Powder
   with Parsley
1 package (1.25 ounces) Lawry's
   Taco Spices & Seasonings
1 can (28 ounces) diced tomatoes,
   undrained
1 can (15 ounces) pinto beans,
   drained
1 can (8¾ ounces) whole kernel
   corn, drained

1 can (4 ounces) diced green chiles,
   drained
1 cup beef broth
½ teaspoon cornstarch
1 pound pork butt *or* beef chuck,
   cooked and shredded
Dairy sour cream (garnish)
Tortilla chips (garnish)
Fresh cilantro (garnish)

In Dutch oven or large saucepan, heat oil. Add onion and Garlic Powder
with Parsley; sauté 2 to 3 minutes until onions are translucent and tender.
Add Taco Spices & Seasonings, tomatoes, beans, corn and chiles; blend well.
In small bowl, gradually blend broth into cornstarch using wire whisk. Stir
into stew. Stir in cooked meat. Bring to a boil, stirring frequently. Reduce
heat to low; simmer, uncovered, 30 minutes, stirring occasionally.
(Or, simmer longer for a thicker stew.) *Makes 8 servings*

PRESENTATION: Garnish each serving with sour cream, tortilla chips and
fresh cilantro, if desired.

VARIATION: Substitute 3 cups cooked, shredded chicken for pork or beef.

Santa Fe Taco Stew

BAJA CORN CHOWDER

A nice Southwest twist on a Midwestern classic.

¼ cup butter or margarine
3 cans (17 ounces *each*) whole
   kernel corn, drained, divided
1 medium red bell pepper, diced
2 cups chicken broth
1 quart half-and-half
1 can (7 ounces) diced green chiles,
   drained

1 package (1.27 ounces) Lawry's
   Spices & Seasonings for
   Fajitas
2 cups (8 ounces) shredded
   Monterey Jack cheese
½ teaspoon Lawry's Seasoned
   Pepper
Hot pepper sauce to taste

In Dutch oven or large saucepan, melt butter. Add one can corn and bell pepper; sauté 5 minutes. Remove from heat. In food processor or blender, place remaining two cans corn and chicken broth; process until smooth. Add to Dutch oven with half-and-half, chiles and Spices & Seasonings for Fajitas. Return to heat. Bring just to a boil, stirring constantly. Remove from heat; blend in cheese, Seasoned Pepper and hot pepper sauce.

Makes 4 to 6 servings

PRESENTATION: Sprinkle with additional Monterey Jack cheese and fresh cilantro, if desired.

FRENCH ONION SOUP

A French favorite.

3 medium onions, thinly sliced and
   separated into rings
2 tablespoons butter or margarine
1 package (1 ounce) Lawry's
   Au Jus Gravy Mix

3 cups water
4 thin slices sourdough French
   bread
   Unsalted butter, softened
4 slices Swiss or Gruyère cheese

In large, deep skillet, sauté onions in 2 tablespoons butter until golden brown. In small bowl, combine Au Jus Gravy Mix and water; add to onions. Bring to a boil. Reduce heat to low; cover and simmer 15 minutes, stirring occasionally. Broil bread on one side until lightly toasted. Turn bread slices over; spread with unsalted butter. Top with cheese; broil until cheese melts.

Makes 4 servings

PRESENTATION: To serve, pour soup into tureen or individual bowls. Top each serving with cheese-covered toast.

HINT: When serving in individual ovenproof bowls, pour soup into bowls; top with a slice of untoasted bread. Top with cheese; place under broiler just until cheese is melted.

INDEX

METRIC CONVERSION CHART

VOLUME MEASUREMENTS (dry)

⅛ teaspoon = 0.5 mL

¼ teaspoon = 1 mL

½ teaspoon = 2 mL

¾ teaspoon = 4 mL

1 teaspoon = 5 mL

1 tablespoon = 15 mL

2 tablespoons = 30 mL

¼ cup = 60 mL

⅓ cup = 75 mL

½ cup = 125 mL

⅔ cup = 150 mL

¼ cup = 175 mL

1 cup = 250 mL

2 cups = 1 pint = 500 mL

3 cups = 750 mL

4 cups = 1 quart = 1 L

VOLUME MEASUREMENTS (fluid)

1 fluid ounce (2 tablespoons) = 30 mL

4 fluid ounces (½ cup) = 125 mL

8 fluid ounces (1 cup) = 250 mL

12 fluid ounces (1½ cups) = 375 mL

16 fluid ounces (2 cups) = 500 mL

WEIGHTS (mass)

½ ounce = 15 g

1 ounce = 30 g

3 ounces = 90 g

4 ounces = 120 g

8 ounces = 225 g

10 ounces = 285 g

12 ounces = 360 g

16 ounces = 1 pound = 450 g

DIMENSIONS

1/16 inch = 2 mm

⅛ inch = 3 mm

¼ inch = 6 mm

½ inch = 1.5 cm

¾ inch = 2 cm

1 inch = 2.5 cm

OVEN TEMPERATURES

250°F = 120°C

275°F = 140°C

300°F = 150°C

325°F = 160°C

350°F = 180°C

375°F = 190°C

400°F = 200°C

425°F = 220°C

450°F = 230°C

BAKING PAN SIZES

Utensil	Size in Inches/ Quarts	Metric Volume	Size in Centimeters
Baking or Cake Pan (square or rectangular)	8×8×2	2 L	20×20×5
	9×9×2	2.5 L	22×22×5
	12×8×2	3 L	30×20×5
	13×9×2	3.5 L	33×23×5
Loaf Pan	8×4×3	1.5 L	20×10×7
	9×5×3	2 L	23×13×7
Round Layer Cake Pan	8×1½	1.2 L	20×4
	9×1½	1.5 L	23×4
Pie Plate	8×1¼	750 mL	20×3
	9×1¼	1 L	23×3
Baking Dish or Casserole	1 quart	1 L	—
	1½ quart	1.5 L	—
	2 quart	2 L	—